THE VOYAGE:
THE POWER OF
ENTREPRENEURSHIP

Julio Zelaya

Show me a worker with great dreams, and I'll give you a man that can change the world. Show me a man without dreams, and I'll give you a simple worker.
— James Cash Penny

CONTENTS

PREFACE

I woke up agitated. My heart was beating strongly, and I was sweating all over. I tried to move, but I couldn't. It's almost as if my head was attached to this strange device that kept me from seeing anywhere else but straight ahead. My mobility was also severely strained. Though I could hardly see in the dimness, I could make out what appeared to be silhouettes of people before me. Were they really people? Were they animals? Were they even real? I wasn't alone in that place; there were countless others. As restricted as I was, I knew it, and though I couldn't move my head freely, I could make out men and women of all ages with an absent-minded glare in their eyes.

I'm not sure what went through my mind, but I knew I had just dreamt something. I had dreamt of being free. I had dreamt with the light of a place different from that cavern. Was my bondage real, or had I imagined it? I believed my dream. I believed it was real.

Slowly, I started to move my feet, my hands. My legs, weakened from being in that same position for what seemed forever, barely responded. Yet, I really wasn't bound. With just a little more effort, my head started to turn, to respond. I started to lose all fear, to take steps. I started being free.

I stumbled my way to other people in that cavern, and to my horror, I discovered that the images were just shadows being projected from the rear of the cave by people holding marionettes over a fire. It was an illusion!

I went up a trail near where I was being held, and I discovered a strange warmth in my countenance. The light gleaming from just outside the cavern blinded me. What was this place? Everything seemed white. In time, I started making out different colors: green, orange, yellow, and red.

For the first time, I felt terror go through me. What should I do? I considered returning to my captivity, for it was easier to stare in one direction than to freely choose where to see. A dreadful anxiety overtook me at the thought of the alternatives before me compared to the security of one same place and the familiar shadows I'd grown used to seeing every day. I slid from anxiety to desolation. This new world was just too open, too unrestrictive. What should I do? Should I go back to the cavern? Yes, that's it! I'll just tell everyone that it was an illusion. That in reality we really were free, and the world was ours. I'll just tell them the dream was reality and invite them to believe in those dreams.

I returned fully energized, already used to the light I had discovered. But then I felt the coldness of the cavern and my eyes had to adjust to the darkness of the past. I descended to where the other prisoners were. I spoke to them, convinced that they would listen to me. It's all been a trick. We can come out. We're free!

Their countenances went from expectant to enraged. Get out of here! You're mad! It's impossible! There's nothing for us out there. Leave us and bother us no more. Their cries became louder. I knew that the situation could quickly turn dangerous, so I exited the cavern and wept. I wept for me. I wept for them. They were free, but they chose to be slaves.

Does this sound familiar? This simple truth narrated by this adaptation of Plato's "Allegory of a Cave" written over 2,400 years ago, is still valid today. Over 70% of people worldwide hate their job, yet they still spend over 80% of their life doing it. They are captive.

Many times we're enslaved, believing that there are no other options for us, that everything they've told us is true. We're just like those prisoners in the cavern. We stop believing that we can move, that we have a choice. Other times, we pay more attention to what we see, to those illusions projected within our perceived enslavement.

Finally, when we embrace the challenge and believe that we can break out, we're terrified by the looming liberty and think about turning back to the comfort of our cavern. And that is where we hear the enticing words of our fellow prisoners inviting us to go on being slaves, convincing us that we've gone mad because of the things we've seen. This is the dilemma every entrepreneur has to face. Dreams are possible, but they require us to dare to believe that another reality does exist and embrace the challenges that usher that liberty in.

Ever since publishing my first book in 2009, *Voyage of an Entrepreneur*, many things have happened. I've grown my business—The Learning Group—to the point of selling it twice. The first time I sold 50% of its shares, buying them all back later, and the second time I sold it entirely.

I also discovered that I needed to be loyal to what I teach and focus my life wholly and entirely on entrepreneurship. This is where EmprendeU was birthed—the organization to which I hope to dedicate the rest of my life. Throughout my walk, I've learned a number of new principles and validated all of the truths set forth in my works. I've come across thousands of entrepreneurs in dozens of cities and countries throughout the world. I've heard their stories. I've received countless emails of stories of both success and failure and gone over many pictograms and life-plans with people. And most of all, I've discovered that the truths set forth in the Voyage are true and current today.

What have I learned throughout these last six years? Indeed, much! What has changed? In one word—*everything*. This is the reason for updating the content in the book and blending and enriching it into a valuable tool that will help you undertake the venture of life. I want to share my newfound knowledge so that we might all leave that cavern behind, to see the light and build the life we were designed for: one of liberty.

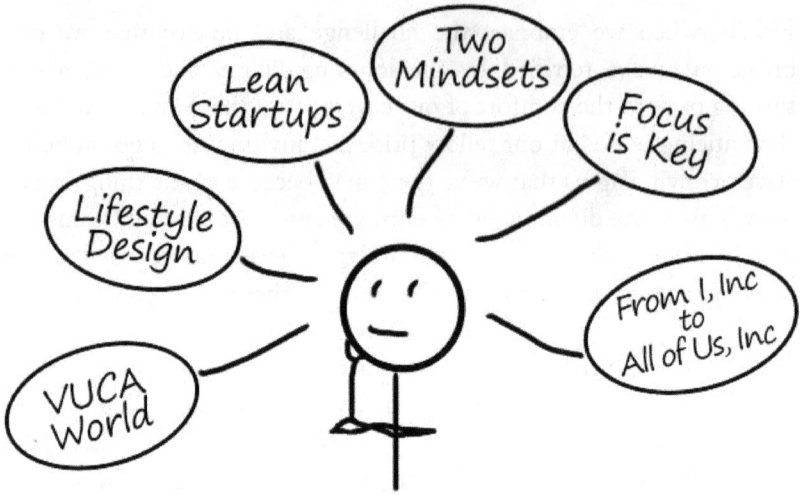

My main lessons throughout this time have been:

The VUCA world

VUCA: Volatility, Uncertainty, Complexity and Ambiguity.

Let's see some examples. Just six years ago:

- Blackberry was one of the leading global companies in the smart phone industry. Today, it struggles for its very existence.
- Whatsapp didn't exist. Today, the application has been sold to Facebook for $22 billion and currently enjoys over 800 million active users.
- Uber, a company threatening traditional taxi service, had not been founded. Today, it has annual sales topping $10 billion.
- Airbnb, an online apartment rental business was just a few months old. Today, it's valued at $20 billion with a business presence in over 34,000 cities and 190 countries.
- Google had an average of 800 billion searches per year. Today, it's in the range of 1.3 trillion searches.

- The iPhone 3GS model had just been released, selling over 7.37 million units in one trimester. Today, they're selling an average of 75 million iPhones per trimester.
- Worldwide Internet coverage increased from 25% to 40%, meaning that close to half of the world's population is now connected online.
- People diagnosed with depression were on the rise. Today it's one of the leading ailments worldwide.
- Facebook had 360 million users. Today, it has almost 1.5 billion users.

Facing these unbelievable realities, I've learned that the world is definitely changing at a rate never to be the same again. Resilience, adaptability, and constant updating are paramount for every entrepreneur.

Lifestyle design

In 2007, Tim Ferris published *The 4-Hour Workweek: Escape 9-5, Live Anywhere, and Join the New Rich*. The book went on to spend 4 years in the New York Times best-seller list and has sold over 1.5 million copies. He introduced a lifestyle design in which he poses the following powerful questions:

- How do you define your ideal lifestyle?
- How do you eliminate what eats your time?
- How do you automate a consistent source of income?
- How do you find freedom?

Tim Ferris puts into doubt the basic concepts of being in one physical location to work or to live. Why should you be in a job you hate, that enslaves you solely for the money that you could easily make another way—perhaps through the use of technology that's readily available.

Today we hear a lot of the "balancing life and work" concept, but I want to take it a step further and think about how to design my life before someone else does it for me.

There are three events that helped me discover that I, together with my key stakeholders, was the one called to define success and how to reach it. The first event was reading Tim Ferris, the second was participating in Aspen's Training Program CALI (Central American Leadership Initiative), and the third was reading Jim Loehr and Tony Schwartz's 2001 article, "The Making of a Corporate Athlete." These findings helped me discover that for far too long I had allowed others to define my life, when in reality my decisions should have been based on the things that would bring joy to both me and my loved ones.

Today, through EmprendeU's design and what I teach on entrepreneurship, I seek to show a new world where quality time forms part of an abundant life and doesn't stand in the way of reaching our purpose. EmprendeU is a business designed to model today's principles, since I can work from home with fellow collaborators from around the globe without ever even meeting them. I can also outsource and automate many key parts of the business; all this without ever overlooking my calling in life.

One of my mentors throughout this process has been Peter Diamandis, founder of XPRIZE and co-founder of Singularity University. Upon meeting him, he said something that totally shifted my perspective in life and in my calling. He said, "Julio, focus on doing something that can impact the lives of a billion people in the next ten years." His challenge helped me start thinking exponentially, and it also caused me to meditate on how the world is currently configured. Can I really impact a billion people without the use of technology? Can I really achieve it without digital systems? Without a doubt, I had to reconfigure the manner in which I operated my business.

During one of the last conversations I had with one of the investors set to purchase The Learning Group, he said, "I'm going to continue with the dream, for as it seems, you've abandoned it." His phrase came after sharing my sentiment of having to sell the business or shut it down. After much self-reflection, I had come to the realization that the structure I had once used to start my business was no longer what my customers were in need of. The idea I founded my business on in 2007 was impossible to manage in 2015 and beyond. On the inside I thought, "I'm going to have to let go of many of my anchors to truly fulfill my dream." In my case, one of these businesses represented an anchor I had in my life. And it was after selling one of these businesses I had founded that I was able to sit down and write these lines, which curiously I'm penning in the Dominican Republic, thereby confirming what Ferris stated of working from anywhere at any time. What is your anchor? What paradigms do we still deem current today? Who will define the lifestyle we wish to enjoy?

I would love to tell you that I discovered these truths on my own; however, it was life's circumstances that led me to break my anchors off. I had decided to sell it all and move to the U.S., due in part to Peter Diamandis' challenge. After selling the business and sharing with a number of close friends and relatives my plans to move to another country, it was then that the unexpected happened: My H1B visa would go to a lottery, never even considering my request or looking at my file.

According to my immigration lawyer, "In the 14 years I've worked in this field, this is the year that I've seen the most requests for that particular type of visa; I'm astounded." Since I've learned that it's best not to force things that don't take place despite our best effort, I focused on my alternatives. I could have seen it in a number of different ways, bad luck perhaps, but since I don't believe in luck, this was indeed the very best gift I could have received. It helped re-evaluate my purpose and the true reasons for wanting to move to America. My goal was still to have greater influence and exponential impact; however, I had to redefine my method of achieving it. Today, I can say that I live in Guatemala, but I'm a citizen of the world, which is what matters most.

Our contemporary situation allows us to design a different lifestyle with a new perspective. I firmly believe that within technology lies the development of a new age of entrepreneurs, since they no longer need to be physically in one place to impact the world.

For example, you can find the best Croatian talent in Guatemala, or the best Guatemalan talent in Croatia. With just a computer or a smart phone, along with an Internet connection, you can do what was once only achievable by the wealthiest corporations. Business has changed, yet entrepreneurship still continues to be a lifestyle.

Lean: A new way of undertaking a venture

Lean startups, a concept made famous by Eric Ries, appear to be the business norm of the day. The question is how to create a "minimal viable product" to launch into the marketplace. The world today allows us to run real-time tests on social networks, websites, Google AdWords and AdSense, Facebook, and all types of online digital platforms.

A man by the name of Jeff Walker created a simple digital product—an email bulletin sharing tips on the stock market. He sent it through his database and 59 seconds later he had closed his first sale. An hour later he had made $8,000, and then earned over $18,000 by the end of the day and $34,000 by the end of the weekend.

The rules have changed, he thought. His best business venture, from home, free of workers, had made him a whopping $106,000 throughout a 7-day period. Today, Jeff Walker has launched a number of million-dollar undertakings, using advertising available to anyone on Google AdWords and directing traffic to his site through Facebook Ads. By using a digital platform, he was able to do what traditionally would have taken dozens of people and a substantial fortune. The world is changing; are your mindset and business keeping up?

New generations are quickly migrating toward a lean chain of thought. Why rent office space if I can do it from home? Why buy a house if I can readily rent one? Stability is no longer measured in property assets but in the functional relationships for which we work hard to develop. The notion of "having things" as indicators of success has evolved into living life more fully, finding satisfaction in people, reaching our purpose, and sharing rather than merely existing. A life full of enriching experiences with the people that matter most to you appears to be the new picture of success.

Today more than ever we can venture as entrepreneurs. I can hire people on platforms such as Freelancer.com. If all I have is $5, I can use Fiverr to sign up people for different parts of my business.

Do you want to publish a book? You can retain most of your earnings by publishing on Amazon Kindle. It'll take you just a few minutes to submit a manuscript in Word, allowing you to instantly sell it in over 70 nations. You can hire a designer on Fiverr who will make your cover for $5 and presto, you're officially an author on Amazon.

Do you want to see your book published worldwide? You can do it right from your home on CreateSpace and distribute it through Ingram. I'm living proof of this idea because, as you read this, I am working on this book with people that I've never met in person because they reside in various countries throughout the world.

These opportunities were virtually non-existent in 2009. Traditional businesses are waning and turning more and more each day into a leaner type of business, relying more heavily on technology and automated processes.

Do you know how I financed this book's first edition? I lost our first house we had already paid in full. This book is a result of all those learning stages. I would never want you to go through everything I went through to become an entrepreneur. The price of doing it the wrong way is too steep.

Two mindsets, two ways of seeing the world

In life, I've learned that there are two ways of seeing the world. No matter what your profession is or what you do in life, I find that people have one of two focuses: a mindset of abundance or a mindset of lack. Where one person envisions abundance, another sees lack. This in turn leads us to react in a certain way and do business in our own peculiar manner.

How do you see the world? Do you see it as a place where "everyone's trying to get me or hurt me" or where "anyone can be my competition" or where "I've got to keep everything for myself," or do you see it as a place where "there's more than enough for everyone?"

Carol Dweck, author of the famous book *Mindset*, clearly illustrates this point. She discovered that 40% of people with a mindset of lack believe that intelligence and personality traits are set at birth and cannot be changed. For example, a person with a high IQ is a genius and a person with a low IQ is lacking intelligence and will always be this way. This is the same lens through which they see their life and undertakings. You'll hear things like, "I was born poor," "I was born in an underdeveloped country," "I come from a dysfunctional family," "I don't have a fatherly or motherly figure," "It's genetics, I can't do anything about it," "This is just how I am," and so on.

Moreover, Dweck also estimates that the amount of people with a mindset of abundance is also about 40% worldwide. People like this believe that a person's intelligence and personality evolves throughout their lifetime and their goal is to improve. All events in their life serve a purpose and what limits them today, with enough hard work and dedication, can change. Common phrases heard in these types of people are, "Everything serves for a purpose in my life," "There's a reason for this," "I can change," "Nothing is set in stone," "I'm the master of my own destiny," "I can build the future I want," and "Sure, I was born this way, but I'm not going to end this way." According to the author, 20% of people are right in the middle with no clear definition between mindsets. Which are you?

Throughout these last six years, there's a saying I've often used with people wanting to start a business: "What do you have right now? Start with that." I invite you to take a self-worth inventory and take stock of what you have. It still amazes me to see the wealth of resources people discover they have when they sit down and write an inventory about themselves, including contacts, access to capital, resources, materials, experiences, and much more. In order to undertake a new venture, you have to use what you have on hand.

Many times we end up having a number of things we've overlooked. If you have limitations, then jot them down to see what options you do have. By looking clearly into the black, we're able to point out the white. That understanding of what you're missing will lead you to fully enjoy abundance and help you better grasp the realities of many people that are facing your same challenges. How do you see yourself today—in abundance or in lack? There is no doubt that whatever we say or believe will end up becoming our reality. Therefore, even in the midst of difficult and trying situations, speak in terms of abundance and express yourself in a positive light.

Focus is the key

During the last few years, I've discovered why Apple cofounder Steve Jobs would always say that his job was to say no. Once you've made strides in achieving your purpose, you need to stay focused. Success draws many things, and many people will always try to steer you toward other businesses and ventures. I've received a number of job offers, investments, partnerships, etc., and I've been diligent in saying no to many of them. With some, I've made the mistake of saying yes when I should have said no.

We live in a world full of distractors, and digital alerts are everywhere: Whatsapp messages, phone calls, Facebook chats, email, Apple Watch reminders, etc. We are more connected and receive more stimuli in our daily lives than ever before in history. The opportunities we've mentioned up until now will be more readily available as time goes on. More than ever, we need to be clear which of these will get a yes and which will get a no.

"Good will always be the enemy of great," says Jim Collins. In other words, sometimes we might have a safe job that we don't like, versus diving into an uncertain business that we might love. The safe job is good; however, that uncertain business might end up being great. The key is to set our focus on what we truly want to do.

I should clear up what I mean by focus. Focus is that which produces consistent results based on our effort. We are constantly drawn away by instant success. Someone recently said to me about the brilliant Guatemalan entrepreneur Luis Von Ahn, "Unbelievable how he made that multi-million dollar investment in Google with his DuoLingo venture." Notwithstanding, we must not overlook the effort Luis had to go through to reach that milestone:

- 2002 Majored in Mathematics and graduated from Duke University Summa Cum Laude
- 2005 Obtained his Ph.D. in Computer Science from Carnegie Mellon University
- 2006 Recipient of the prestigious MacArthur Fellowship Award
- 2009 Sold reCaptcha to Google
- 2009–2015 Received a number of awards

Was his success really instantaneous, or was it a result of continual and consistent work, focused on a pathway of excellence?

I've known entrepreneurs who just a few months into their startup say, "I'm going to go back to my day job because nothing is turning out right." To say that nothing is working after just a few months in any venture is pretty drastic. People that have transcended haven't done so on their first try, but after multiple, consistent learning stages

Is Angry Birds a success story? After viewing its over 2 billion downloads, there's no question it's a definite yes. However, let's analyze this case more closely to see that Rovio's success didn't come until after 50 different game versions that never really took off. Actually, Angry Birds is the 52nd version, and it didn't come out until 6 years later when 3 young people from Helsinki, Finland decided to go into business together in 2009. The key lies in sustained focus. Entrepreneurship isn't a sprint, but it's a marathon.

From I, Inc. to Us, Inc.

In *Voyage of an Entrepreneur*'s first edition, I spoke about I, Inc.—that business we start when we first discover our calling. During these last few years, I've discovered how that first undertaking becomes Us, Inc. when we invite others to join us in the voyage. I also discovered that we must shift our perception from merely being successful to actually transcending. I've awakened to a collective awareness and discovered that whatever we do will have a great impact in our surroundings.

I know this might sound logical, but all too often we set our eyes on ourselves and not on those around us, overlooking the fact that what we do will have a direct impact on our planet and our community. Indeed, whatever we do will impact our generation. This is where our call to undertake a venture should turn into an All of Us, Inc. In other words, to reproduce in others the same desire to break free of that bondage, come out of that cavern, and transcend, to go beyond those two vital needs of people and profit and embrace a project that incorporates sustainability within it. One indicator that we are transitioning into that All of Us, Inc. mindset is by answering the question, "How can we impact a billion people in the next ten years by taking on any of mankind's challenges?"

The voyage of an entrepreneur is current today

My main lesson these last couple of years has been that the principles I laid out in *Voyage of an Entrepreneur* are still valid, real, and powerful today.

During this season, I've seen the birth of foundations, restaurants, magazines, smart phone apps, online games, simulators, professional service enterprises, and startups by close associates, as well as by the competition. I have also witnessed the birth of corporate startups where managers of important transnational corporations discovered their calling and the means to achieve it, within their enterprise. Believe me when I tell you it has been both exciting and gratifying.

I have seen how innovative projects, prototypes, and the launching of new units are the means to perpetuate that entrepreneurial spirit by which companies are founded. This is a great way to retain the individuals that had already resigned but were still around. I also discovered that emotional resignation and physical permanency are commonly found in corporations and that sharing these principles have become an effective mechanism to boost internal commitment.

I have shared these principles with hundreds of thousands of people through onsite workshops, through EmprendeU.com, and through the digital and magazine publications of *Voyage of an Entrepreneur*. I've had the privilege many times of hearing the words, "Now I am doing what I love." It's the greatest gift I've received because once again I believe in my dreams and in the transforming power of ideas. I get excited every time I see a person that's discovered their calling and shifted their passion and talent toward it. There are hundreds of thousands of people leaving that cavern, inspiring others to be a better version of themselves. My desire is that this new version of *The Voyage* helps you in dreaming again and in undertaking that incredible voyage of building the business of your life.

Julio Zelaya
Santo Domingo, Dominican Republic
June 20, 2015

WHY READ THIS BOOK

Reason #1: Statistics don't favor the unprepared.

(Here is a table taken from Scott Shane's book, *The Illusions of Entrepreneurship*)

Myths and Realities of Undertaking a New Business Venture
Shane, Scott (2008). *The Illusions of Entrepreneurship*. USA: Yale University Press.

Element	Myth or Reality	Evidence
Entrepreneurs tend to start businesses in the service industry.	Myth	It's estimated that only 35–40% of new startups are in the service industry.
Entrepreneurs start businesses where there isn't much competition.	Myth	The majority of entrepreneurs get involved in industries filled with many similar businesses.
Entrepreneurs start businesses in industries that tend to be easier.	Reality	The majority of entrepreneurs start businesses in sectors that are easier to enter into; however, the rate of failures in these industries is higher than those of more complex ones.
Entrepreneurs start businesses in industries they've worked in before.	Reality	45% of start-ups are in a field that an entrepreneur has already worked in.
There are psychological traits that set apart entrepreneurs from those who are not.	Myth	There is no conclusive evidence showing significant differences between entrepreneurs and non-entrepreneurs.

The main reason for anyone starting a business is to make money.	Myth	The main reason for people going into business for themselves is because they no longer like working for someone else.
The average age of an entrepreneur is 20 years old.	Myth	The most common age for starting businesses is in the 35–44 year range.
Greater work experience increases the likelihood for a person to go into business.	Reality	Work experience increases the probability of starting your own business.
A better education increases the possibility of going into business for yourself.	Reality	Evidence suggests that getting an education increases the possibility of starting your own business. However, greater academic degrees do not raise the probability of becoming an entrepreneur.
Entrepreneurs offer unique products and services when they launch a business.	Myth	Only 10% of all new businesses offer a unique product or service not offered by other companies.
New businesses create employment.	Myth	76% of new businesses don't hire anyone. They just have one employee, including the founder.
Entrepreneurs believe the business will make them more money than their current job.	Myth	33% of entrepreneurs do not believe their new business will ever be large enough to take the place of their current job.
Entrepreneurs hardly ever include formal research with their business idea.	Reality	Generally speaking, new entrepreneurs make little to no formal research, nor hardly collect any information for their business idea.
Every entrepreneur starts their company with a clear business idea.	Myth	40% of all entrepreneurs launch their business before having a clear business idea.
All businesses start with a clear and structured business plan.	Myth	Most entrepreneurs take an average of 18 months to write down their business plan.

Most companies are founded by a group of partners.	Myth	Approximately 50–60% of all new businesses are founded by an individual.
The main source of capital for new businesses is derived from external investors.	Myth	The majority of undertakings are started off with the founder's savings.
Having initial capital available increases the probabilities of starting a business.	Myth	Studies have shown that people who win the lottery or receive an inheritance don't necessarily go into business.
Common sources of financing for a new business are credit cards.	Reality	Approximately 28.3% of startups have been funded with resources stemming from credit cards.
Family and friends are a great source of financing.	Myth	Barely 7.8% of new businesses are founded with funding from family or friends.
The majority of new businesses are successful.	Myth	Only 45% of new businesses make it past the first 5 years and an even lower 30% of them make it past the first 10.
Entrepreneurs are happier than those who work for someone else	Reality	Studies have shown that people who go into business for themselves are happier than those who work for others.
Business people make more than employees working for someone else.	Myth	On average, a businessman makes 35% less than they would be working for someone else. After 25 years of being a businessman, the majority make 25% less than they would working for others.
Entrepreneurs work fewer hours than employees do.	Myth	On average, entrepreneurs work 15.4 hours more per week.

I consider myself an optimist, yet I must admit that upon reading these statistics I was slightly fearful to go into business for myself. Do you know why I included this table? To prepare you and help you be a part of the select minority of successful business people. The good news is that there are studies that highlight what successful business people do. If you choose to apply the advice in the following pages, you'll greatly increase your likelihood of success.

Reason #2: Over 95% of all business people don't know the top 5 reasons for companies going under. (But now *you* will.)

1. **Erratic Strategies.** Very few businesses enjoy clear strategic planning. It's common to find erratic, shifting behaviors within the company's strategies resulting in confusion with customers, suppliers, and fellow workers.

2. **Family-owned businesses lacking structure.** It's common to find businesses run by two or more family members lacking a corporate charter or a professional administrative board. The consequences of this are inner bickering, the perception of "I'm working harder than you," and a lack of real performance.

3. **Unskilled entrepreneurial founders.** It's common to find entrepreneurs that have gone broke from not seeking professional advice or for not putting together professional work teams. They launch startups without any preparation, more for the thrill of starting a business or simply the need of doing something, anything.

4. **Lack of controls.** It's common for new businesses to go belly up because of theft or cash flow issues. This is due in no small part to a lack of controls.

5. **Lack of liquid assets.** When you first start a business, you tend to draw a highly optimistic future of it and not a gloomy one that takes into account unforeseen recurring costs and extended payment times from customers. Cash flow, and the lack thereof, is a common cause of failure in new businesses. Do you want to be sure that you have enough cash flow? Plan for no sales during the first six months. Multiply your fixed expenses by six,

and you'll know the approximate amount required to start your business.

You must like the business, not love it! Love is blind, often keeping you
from making good decisions.
– Walter de la Cruz (Cafe Barista Founder)

Those who fail to plan, plan to fail.
– George Hewell

Reason #3: You will dedicate 80% of your life to what you do. Discovering your purpose is worth not having to be part of the 70% of the population that hate what they do.

This book deals with one of the most important decisions you'll ever face in life: how to live out your calling by opening up a business or being part of the staff of one. It's a vital decision because to a certain degree it's designed to influence your success in the spiritual, personal, family, and social realms of your life. Just think about it, you spend more hours at work than in any other activity. Our lifetime is too unique and limited to squander it on things we were never designed to do.

There are three ways to view your work every day:

1. Some people see it as only labor, the means to receive some sort of payment.

2. Other people see it as a career, a process to continue advancing in life, hiking the hill of job-hunting, in search for another one with better benefits.

3. And finally, there are those that view it as a call or a purpose. It's something stronger and deeper. It defines what we were born for according to a greater plan.

No matter what you do every day, you're going to fit into one of these categories. Whether you're an executive, teacher, spiritual leader, writer, janitor, cook, taxi driver, construction worker, or engineer. There's a vision of life in everyone that fits into these dimensions. Which one are you? Which one would you like to be?

How do you wake up every morning? Do you go, "Oh, how horrible, I hate this dreadful job, but at least I get paid." Or do you say, "I love doing what I enjoy and what I'm good at!" This last statement, although simple as it might seem, will set your mood and humor for the rest of the day. It's a powerful clue to know if you're really doing what you were called to. I like something Steve Jobs said in his speech at Stanford: "If I've been getting up now for a number of days doing something I don't like, then it's time for a change."

> *Live life seeking to fulfill many of the things you've dreamed about,*
> *and you won't ever have time left to feel bad.*
> *– Richard Bach*

I recently had the opportunity of completing a certification in one of the most world-renowned universities on entrepreneurship—Babson College. During an engaging conversation with Len Schlensinger, its president, he shared the following thought. "What would I say at a press conference if during my tenure as president at Babson we were to fall in our rankings after being number one for fifteen years straight?"

He shared how that was his first great challenge when he became president. After talking about it and discussing it with the various teams in the institution, he noticed something that completely shifted the way he viewed the problem. "We were more focused on the final result (being number one) rather than enjoying what we were doing right now, which was teaching and relishing the undertaking as a means of changing the world."

He also added that a source of inspiration for this change was due to the strategy employed by the famous rock band, the Grateful Dead. They were the first to do something that was unheard of for a musical band. At their concert entrances, instead of searching people to make sure they didn't sneak in recorders or video cameras, they reserved preferential seating in the first few rows for them to get a better recording of the concert. They encouraged them to bring their recording devices and make the event a personal experience for them.

When asked why they took this approach, which might greatly impact their album sales, they simply replied, "We're the only band to really put our customers and fans first." Thanks to the band's attitude, they always hit their sales goals.

Len points out that Babson College had stopped focusing on the goal and focused more on the process that would ultimately lead them to achieve that goal. He urged me to start thinking in a revolutionary way, "Why compete to be the best when you can simply be unique?" And there's no doubt that it's working for them. Their educators enjoy teaching and their students revel in the entire experience. They are doing what they love to do.

On the other hand, I also have had the privilege of working with a number of boards and managerial groups of corporations throughout the region. On one occasion, I recall being impacted by an organization that, despite it being one of the largest in the world, enjoying key positions in their industry, and having one of the most sophisticated compensation and talent-development systems around, had many of their executives expressing how they would rather be doing something else. Consequently, this isn't an isolated incident. It hardly ever is in the businesses I work with.

Many people, including CEOs, seem to lose that spark in their eye and start asking, "Am I really doing what I want to do in life?" Some people have said to me, "I'm too old for a change." Others say, "You don't understand; we wouldn't be able to keep up with that lifestyle." Curiously, it was the same syndrome that Babson College was going through with everyone focusing on "not losing what we've got" instead of "I'll have what I want if I just start doing what I like."

Doing what you like is a reflection of your calling in life. It's the inner force that motivates you in secret. It's that problem that you alone can solve. Simon Sinek asserts, "There are leaders, and then there are those who lead. The first group have a title, but the second group are those that inspire and move the world." The question you need to ask yourself is, "Are you willing to do what you really desire to do? Will you do what you should do? Living an extraordinary life is a result of making decisions that seem ordinary but that lead us to become the best we can be. And these in turn open up the door to balance and realization.

You should read this book because we are all dreamers with a vision for the future, and we all have a desire to live life to the fullest. This book is designed for people that are determined to reinvent themselves and do extraordinary things. It's designed for people that wish to impact their life, their family, their job, and their nation by using their talent to create a better world.

This isn't a motivational book; it's a book based on findings that span a number of different disciplines, such as entrepreneurship, administrative science, social psychology, anthropology, philosophy, and human performance. In addition, it's a journey of my own experiences working around the world with all types of people and businesses in both the private and public sectors, as well as with for-profit and non-profit organizations.

Furthermore, it's also a voyage through our own lives to ask ourselves powerful questions that can determine if we really are on the right path or if a change of direction is required.

This book is designed for people with a mindset of abundance and growth, as well as for those with a slightly rigid mindset. It's designed to enrich your discovery of the passionate world of business, of dreams, and of wholesome realities. You can do anything you set your mind to, but first you need to learn some key things to undertake any venture—and that's what this book is for.

How is this book structured?

I, Inc.

How to discover what I was made to do in life.

We, Inc.

How to invite other people to share in my calling and how to get it started.

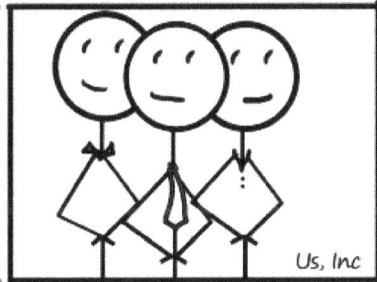

All of Us, Inc.

How to turn my calling into something that transcends and causes an exponential impact.

I, Inc.

1

The Choice to Undertake

An ounce of experience is worth more than a pound of theory.
– Benjamin Franklin

"You don't have what it takes to be in the Liverpool Cathedral Choir," were the words that marked a young man's life. He loved singing, but he hated singing lessons. Would he choose to believe those words? No. Instead, he chose to do something about it. In fact, he was so determined that he founded his own institute for musical talent development, the Liverpool Institute for Performing Arts. Who am I talking about? No less than the most widely successful composer in history—Paul McCartney—with 60 gold records and over 100 million albums sold. Over 2,000 artists have sung versions of his song *Yesterday*, turning it into the most widely sung, copyrighted musical piece in the world. It's this and many other examples that press us to think, "Who's going to define the destiny of the most important business of your life, the one we call I, Inc.?"

I love reading. I've been an avid reader since I was a young child, and the books I enjoy most are the "how to" ones, those with a practical application in life. It's easy to write about the "what," describing and defining something, but it's much harder to write about how to carry it out. For example, I can say a lot about business, but then you might ask, "All right, but how do I do it? How do I really reach what I want in life?" Those are the questions that matter. In order to write the "how to," one must first experience it to be able to convey the lessons learned and to sift through what we should do and not do differently again—contrasting theory with reality. As you might imagine, writing about being an entrepreneur comes with its own set of challenges.

First, in business there are no formulas for success. There is always an element of variability that makes each case unique. Second, I would be gullible to think I've lived and experienced enough in life to give you magical formulas that can apply to every business endeavor and setting. Nonetheless, being a reader and businessman has led me to the conclusion that today we have less time for reading. Furthermore, what we are actually seeking are effective tools to apply, rather than lengthy portions of theory to pore over. This is the reason for this updated version of *Voyage of an Entrepreneur*, which I have filled with tools, practical applications, and best practices for your business endeavor.

Start by answering the following questions: When, in what area, and how should I plan my business venture? We'll tackle these questions, and we'll design a consistent and convincing business plan followed by describing the different hurdles a businessperson needs to overcome.

If you already have your own business or are thinking of starting one, then this book is for you. The tools set forth here will help you start or grow your business with the highest probability of success. It will expose you to the best practices worldwide and the ones proven most successful.

Business has been a passion of mine as long as I can remember, especially when it comes to teaching about it. I've dedicated my life to sifting through my own successes and failures, as well as those of thousands of companies and business people I've come to know personally and throughout my research. My calling is to aid you in recovering those dreams and help you reach them. I'm going to challenge you to ask yourself time and again, "What am I doing today to make my dreams a reality and be the best version of myself I can be?" Together, let's embark on this life-changing journey for you, and those around you, known as the *Voyage of an Entrepreneur*.

Only those daring to go far will ever really know how far they will go.
– T.S. Eliot

About dreams and inner talk

Every business is birthed from a dream, but prior to that we need a dreamer. Do you remember your childhood and how you used to dream? You probably dreamt the impossible, perhaps about being a fireman, an astronaut, a scientist, a doctor helping to cure many people, or a policeman keeping them safe. But what happens when we grow up? We start hearing people's logical reasons for not becoming what we once dreamt of, and we settle for living someone else's life.

Have you ever thought about how often we live someone else's dream? We live the dream that our father, our mother, our spouse, our children, our friends, our bosses, or our neighbors want, and we leave for last the dream that God has entrusted us with, the one that truly is yours and that you alone have the power to carry out. The decision lies in your hands. There are some people who choose to strive for their dreams, and others who sadly go through life as a routine, living someone else's dreams.

I'll never forget an experience I had once with a high executive. The manager of a human resources department had called me and said, "Julio, maybe you can help him." She shared how many in the company thought of him as a tyrant and an ogre, and how that people would literally flee from his presence. Just the mere fact of meeting him piqued my interest, for this was a person with a long track record and multiple articles in business magazines and newspapers. Moreover, the opportunity of helping him find his passion for work was even more exhilarating for me.

When I got to the office, the HR manager just said, "Good luck!" and started making her way out. "Aren't you going to go in with me," I said?

"No way" was the reply. "He doesn't even know what the meeting is about, but I sure hope you can help him."

Hmm, thanks for the heads up.

I walked into his office, and there he was, sitting at his desk, deeply engaged in his computer. He didn't even bother looking up to greet me and just mumbled, "Sit down." I took my seat with a sense of expectation of what was about to happen.

"All right, what do you want? You've got five minutes," he said.

"It's a pleasure meeting you. I would just like you to help me with a few questions. I'm doing some research on entrepreneurship, and you're a very influential person. I would love to be able to document your success story."

"There are no secrets, just work hard and that's all" he grumbled back. "Anything else I can do for you?"

It was obvious that I was getting nowhere that way, so I tried asking him a few questions. "If you could only give your children one word of advice for their lives, what would it be?" I continued.

"I told you already—work hard, no shortcuts," he hammered back.

"And what did you dream of doing as a child?" I continued.

That was the question that shifted everything. His face immediately changed. A deafening silence fell in the room. He left his computer, turned his chair, and stared at me with a chilling glare and it felt like decades went by in only a few seconds. His stare remained fixed, and you could hear a mosquito buzzing in the background. For a moment, I thought he would holler at me and run me out of the office. I thought of a thousand different scenarios in that moment. But then he stood up and slowly made his way to a closet he had there in his office. This is when I really started to worry. *Would he take me to Narnia?* I thought, trying to find some humorous relief. He stood in front of the closet and after a few more seconds he finally opened it.

Inside was an old dusty guitar, and you could tell it had been around for quite a while. He took it in his hands and with a sigh of somberness headed back toward me. "This is what I always dreamt of doing one day," he said. "But my dad on his deathbed told me, 'I hope you take over this business, son, because I could never forgive you for not continuing what took me so much hard work to build.' So I obeyed him."

How could this executive ever come to value what he did every day if it always served as a reminder of the reason he could never pursue what he really wanted in life? In time, we became friends, and I'm happy to say that he's learning how to play that guitar. Someone else is leading the business. He finally discovered someone in the company that would love that job, and both he and the business are much better off.

Kids' wisdom

What did you dream of as a child? I recommend having a notebook ready as you read this book to complete some interesting exercises as we go along. Jot down your childhood dreams, and please be as specific as possible.

I wasn't more than eight years old when I mixed a number of ingredients in a jar and labeled it "mediopetril." Of course, it was a foul-tasting concoction with Vaseline, colorants, Play-Doh, water, and other items I had found around my home. I remember telling my parents, "I've invented something that will cure everything."

Back then, my dad was working for a pharmaceutical company, and I recall asking him for an appointment at his company to present my invention. He asked me about the performance tests, and I answered, "I tried it on my turtles, and they all died, but that's just because it's not made for animals. That's why I would like a meeting at your company."

Just picture the scene. It was a critical point in my life, and without hesitation, my dad assured me, "You can count on that meeting, but you'll need to be better prepared." My mom showed her support as well.

Days went by, and I finally heard my dad say, "Tomorrow's the big day; I got you a meeting with the general managers." With all the excitement an eight-year-old could muster, I put my suit on, readied my dreadful potion, gathered some drawings I had put together, and headed off with my dad to work. Just like he said, there was a group of managers waiting for me in the boardroom.

I went through my presentation without a single one of them chiding or looking down on me. I'm sure my dad had prepped them ahead of time. At the end of the meeting, one of them took off his watch and handed it to me along with a book he had taken out of his brief-case. I'll never forget the words he said, for they marked my life. "I'm giving you this watch as an initial capital investment to follow your dream. Read this book, *The Greatest Salesman in the World*, to prepare yourself even more."

They were saying that I was headed in the right direction, to con-tinue my research, and one day I would get my big shot. I never felt one least bit that it was impossible. When I got back home, I cele-brated that important business meeting with my parents. Never for-get, we all have the power to free or kill our dreams.

Why have I called this work, *Voyage of an Entrepreneur*? Because I want you to remember that the most important part of any new ven-ture is enjoying the journey itself. The destination isn't the only thing that matters, but also enjoying the process of getting there. That's why we talk so much about the wisdom found in children. Like them, we must simply enjoy the processes we go through in life.

My children's births were events that marked my life. To be honest, it was also one of the most frightening events of my life. Seeing them so defenseless and totally dependent on me gave me anxiety. "What if I'm not a good role model?" However, little by little, my love for them started displacing all of that fear, allowing me to develop a healthy, fatherly relationship. My two children, Juan Ignacio and Natalia, have helped me recover the wonder of it all and have allowed me to see life through a new set of eyes. Here are six lessons these two teachers have taught me.

1. **Children are humble.** They know that they need help. In time, we forget how to be little, how to be humble. (Humility comes from the Latin *humilis*, which is related to being little.) We forget to acknowledge that sometimes we are defenseless, vulnerable, and in search of direction. We forget that a tiny microscopic virus or bacteria can kill us. We seek validation, not for who we are, but for what we do or what we possess. Are you still being humble (little) today?

2. **Children aren't seeking to be happy, they simply are.** In time, we forget that happiness is a state of mind, not a goal. We grow up, and we set happiness as our highest goal in life when we could be it right now in this very moment. We fall prey to thinking we'll be happy "When I have this amount of money, when I have this type of job, when something else happens, etc." Are we really happy now, today? What's keeping you from living in that state of gratitude and appreciation for what you already have?

3. **Children don't know about limitations, just possibilities.** In time, we forget that wanting to be an astronaut is possible. We turn into adults, and instead of thinking of what we can be, we start believing what others say we should be. If they tell us it can't be done, we hold on to it more than the world of possibilities we used to live in as a child. Are you seeing the opportunities around you today?

4. **Children don't worry about tomorrow; they just live passionately today.** In time, we start postponing the enjoyment of our present in exchange for worrying about tomorrow. We forget to play and take pleasure in the free things life has for us and instead decide that we'll "spend more time with our family when we get around to it." Are you making the time to live life—I mean *really* live it?

5. **Children aren't looking for a special moment to show their affection; they just do it.** In time, we forget to say, "I love you" or "I'm sorry," and instead we look for the perfect moment to do so. The simplest of words can have the same effect now and today. Have you recently told your loved ones how much you love them?

6. **Children don't doubt their provision, for they know that it will always come.** In time, we forget that we can have faith, that we can trust in God and all of our needs will be met. Do you have faith in God's provision today?

> *He called a little child to him and placed the child among them.*
>
> *And he said, "Truly I tell you, unless you change and become like little children, you will never enter the kingdom of heaven.*
>
> *Therefore, whoever takes the lowly position of this child is the greatest in the kingdom of heaven.*
>
> *(Matthew 18:2-4, KJV)*

We must learn from children. We must be grownups and children at the same time when it comes to dreaming, to having faith, and to visualizing a world of possibilities. Choose to be a person and an entrepreneur of purpose that has chosen to go back to the basics and view life through the refreshing eyes of optimism.

Perhaps it's because of this positive attitude that it's easier to venture into a new undertaking at a certain age, such as when you're young or when you at least feel young. You see, age really isn't connected to a number, but to the focus we choose to have in life. If you haven't lost your wonder, if you're still excited about living life to the fullest, and if you still believe and are willing to change, then you are still young.

Let's analyze this notion about dreams more deeply from another perspective. What do you tell your children when they share their dreams with you? What do you tell your spouse when they share their dream? What do you tell yourself about your own dreams?

Reverend Milton Wright, bishop of the Church of the United Brethren in Christ in Iowa, had a particular vision for mankind in the 20th century. He was very clear about it during an interview with the head of a university from the eastern coast of the U.S. The rector asked, "Is the world going to end?"

The reverend assured him, "Absolutely, I'm convinced of it. The end isn't far. If we analyze things, everything that had to be discovered was discovered already. Man has already invented everything that can be invented. This is a clear sign that we've reached the end of times."

"Well, I think mankind will soon learn how to fly," continued the rector with a slight tone of fear in his voice.

"Nonsense," raged the reverend. "If God had meant us to fly, he would have given us wings. Please don't blaspheme. Humans will never fly—ever! Flying is reserved for the birds and the angels."

Bishop Milton had two boys, Orville and Wilbur. Two children that fortunately had a different vision in life than their father. And so the Wright brothers were the ones who first invented the plane and helped fulfill mankind's dream of flying. We don't know what their father might have told them as children, but if he was as blatantly negative as he was in his interview, we can safely assume that the brothers must have used their father's words as the tailwind to make their dream a reality.

Program your words and beliefs

In order to analyze yourself as an entrepreneur, you must first inspect your word choice. Are you generally an optimist or a pessimist? What do others have to say about you? Would you say you normally have words of comfort or of bad news? These questions have a scientific foundation behind them to achieve your dreams. We're going to see more about this later on.

In the meanwhile, I want to share two valuable thoughts. A pessimist is a person that even with light will only see shadows. An optimist sees how close we are to something; a pessimist sees how far. There's an interesting scripture in the Bible that says, "From the fruit of the mouth one's stomach is satisfied; the yield of the lips brings satisfaction. Death and life are in the power of the tongue, and those who love it will eat its fruits. (Proverbs 18:20–21, KJV) You must learn to reprogram your mind to only speak positive words. Our mouth has power.

Would you like another reason to reprogram your thought patterns and your belief system? World-renowned coach Anthony Robbins sums these principles up in the following diagram:

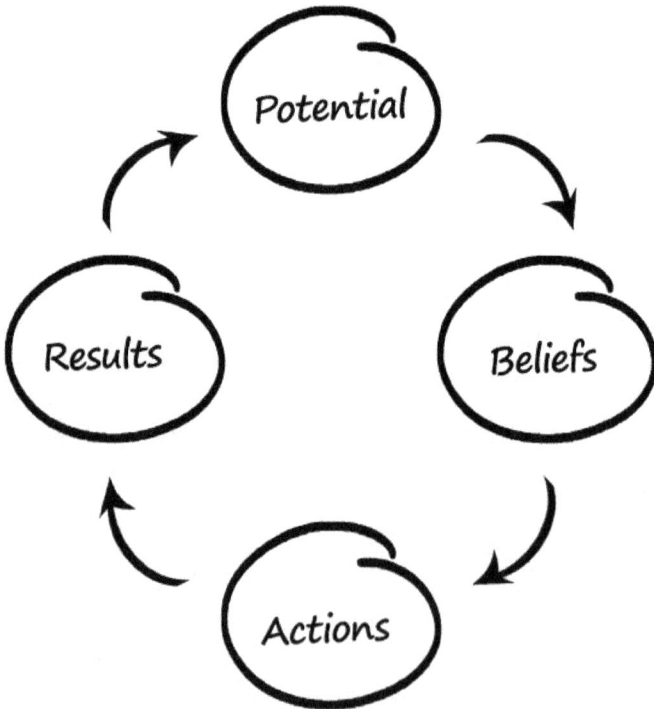

If you believe you have low potential, that in turn will cause you to believe that you can't achieve much in life. You'll become mediocre in whatever you do and never seek after excellence. You'll obtain poor results, confirming the perception you had about your potential. This in turn will reaffirm your beliefs, and you will end up in a never-ending cycle.

On the other hand, if you believe you have unlimited potential, then you'll also believe that you can achieve great things in life. This will lead you to perform everything with excellence. You'll get great results, which will confirm your original perception about yourself. It'll reaffirm your beliefs and the cycle will never end.

What are your results like? Perhaps it's time to examine the perception you have of your potential and your beliefs so that both your actions and your results will be in positive alignment.

Think of the greatest dream you've ever had, and write the thoughts that automatically come to mind about it. What do those thoughts tell you? Do they encourage you to press on, or do they tell you that you're off? One of the greatest things about the brain is that it can't tell the difference between fantasy and reality, therefore your brain stores and interprets everything you say as if it were true. For example, if you think, "I'm not going to make it," then your brain stores that. But if you think, "I am going to make it," then your brain stores that instead.

You can only make your dreams a reality to the degree that you speak about them in a positive light. Let's say that you're studying for a test. You might say, "I'm not going to fail it." However, it would be better to say, "I'm going to pass it," or "I'm going to ace it." Thinking this way helps program you with a positive outlook in life, and your brain stores it as, "You're going to pass this test."

If you choose to become an entrepreneur, your greatest battle will be in your mind. That is the reason why the first thing I recommend is to train in positive thinking.

Every year, I speak to thousands of people in my workshops, and one of the questions I usually ask is, "What is one of your dreams?" I've noticed five types of answers.

1. Those that speak about them in a tone of resignation with statements such as, "I'm too old for it," "I don't have enough money," or "I stopped believing in them already."

2. Those that speak about other people's dreams. "My dream is to see my children graduate from college," or "I dream of being able to give something back to my parents."

3. Those that speak about their dreams in a belittling manner. "Sure, I'd like something on the side," or "I know I can't hope for much, but eh, I'll do something."

4. Those that speak about their immediate dreams or long-term ones. "I'd love to pay off my house," or "I'd like to move up the corporate ladder."

5. Those that speak of their dream to change the world. "I dream of seeing my country transformed," or "I dream of all the people in my nation learning to read and write."

Which of these do you believe is most common? Interestingly, it's a combination of the first three. There are few people that actually want something greater than themselves, even if they do have the capacity and calling to do so. When they dare to dream of the possibilities, they automatically activate a self-correction mechanism that tells them, "But you don't have the money," "But you're already married with children," "but..."

The people that reach their dreams are those that always talk and meditate on them in a positive light, as if they've already achieved them. I want you to take your notebook and write positive thoughts about your dream.

Peter Diamandis was born in 1961 in the Bronx. His parents, Greek immigrants, were involved in the medical field. However, his passion for outer space was clearly evident even as a small child. By the age of eight, he was giving talks to his friends of what it would be like to explore the universe. At the age of twelve, he won a contest for a systems design that could launch three rockets at the same time. He graduated from MIT with a degree in astronautics and from Harvard as a doctor. He then worked on a number of research projects for NASA on outer space.

"My dream has always been to explore space," he'd tell us in the talk I met him at. "However, there were a number of obstacles." Using all of his contacts and a deep, relentless desire to solve the issue of space exploration, he decided to create a competition inspired by the history of Charles Lindbergh's, The Spirit of St. Louis. During a news conference, he announced a $10 million reward for whoever could submit the best technology to privately transport passengers into space. The competition, called XPRIZE, was birthed on May 18th, 1996.

When asked about the prize money, Peter would reply, "I don't have it yet, but I know it'll flow once we get some ideas rolling." Many people said no to his investment initiative. Peter told me that dozens of CEOs turned down the opportunity to chip in for the prize money. Finally, after reading a story of a young executive who had become a billionaire after selling her company and who, just like him, dreamt of going into space, they joined forces to form what is now known as Ansari XPRIZE, in honor of her family.

Today, many years later, the winning team sold the technology to Richard Branson, and the Virgin Galactic business was founded. Peter is on the board, and they are on the threshold of making his dream a reality. Did you once dream of being an astronaut, but everyone said you were crazy? They said the same thing to Peter dozens of times. But today, he's turning it into a reality for all of mankind.

The brain secretary: The reticular activating system

Have you ever noticed how people who reach their dreams speak passionately about them? They see an opportunity to share that vision and make it a reality with every person they come across. Did you know there's a scientific explanation behind this?

I want to invite you to do an experiment with me. Pay close attention to all of the sounds around you. You'll quickly notice there are sounds you hadn't picked up before: a bird chirping outside, traffic on the street, someone clicking on a keyboard, the air conditioning unit humming in your office, etc. Focus on all of those sounds that were there, yet you hadn't perceived them before. Surprised?

Now, I want to challenge you to a second experiment. Read the following question carefully: Have you ever noticed how many white cars there are in your city? If you meditate on this question for a moment, I guarantee that the minute you step outside, you'll notice how many white cars there are that you'd never noticed before. You'll start seeing them everywhere.

Now why does this happen? Our brain has a function known as the reticular activating system or as my mentor Sharon Bowman puts it, the "brain secretary."

It's designed to focus on important things and block out the rest. If you weren't able to block out certain stimuli, you'd live in a constant state of alertness, hindering you from being productive. You would listen to every single sound without ever differentiating which ones matter and which ones don't. Are you starting to understand why it's so important to talk about your dreams? People who reach their dreams always talk about them for three main reasons:

1. They program their brains for it. To the extent that they sort their goals and share them, their reticular activating system compares their dream to their environment and says, "This will help you achieve it." If you've set your mind that your dream is to open up the best restaurant in the nation, everything you

experience will become input or raw material for that dream until you make it a reality.

2. You start forming a network of supporters. By sharing your dream with others, people with similar desires start connecting with you to support it. People love it when someone reaches their dream. In fact, some of the most successful people in the world have focused on helping others reach their dreams in the process of reaching their own. If you talk about your restaurant, all those who meet you will know that it's your dream and when someone sees something that can add value to it, they'll surely let you know.

3. Finally, and perhaps the most important reason of all, is because you acquire a commitment that demands consistency. One of the most undesired traits in a person is inconsistency in their words and deeds. If you talk about your dream, you'll commit even more to achieving it. More often than not, people keep from sharing their dreams because deep down there is a subtle fear of failure. But you need to make up your mind as to what's more important: fighting for your dream or settling for someone else's. There's no doubt in my mind—it's better to fight for your own dream.

Those who have known me since childhood know exactly what I'm talking about. My classmates in school knew that I loved to study and teach. I used to participate in every competition possible in the following areas: speaking, writing, and declamation. Ever since my early years, I always dreamt of one day teaching and writing. Sharing my dreams has given me the opportunity to write books with authors such as Steve Forbes and Brian Tracy. It's also granted me the opportunity to meet a number of people who have helped me along the process, such as Dave Ulrich, Sir Ken Robinson, Jack Welch, Mark Victor Hansen, Jim Collins, Stephen Covey, Ram Charan, Ken Blanchard, Peter Diamandis, and Verne Harnish. We will draw nearer to what we want if we are as specific as possible in what we long for and if we share it with the world. Everyone else might say we're crazy—right up until the moment we achieve it.

SMART

Write a detailed description of your dream(s). Be as specific as possible.

So far, we've seen that to reach your dream it's important to share it with other people. This will help you be even more committed to it. It will keep you focused and help build a network of supporters around it.

Another important ingredient to reach your dream is visualizing and living it. Here's an example: Would you like to have a larger home for your family? If the answer is yes, then I urge you to go visit the type of house you would like to live in. Walk through it, feel it, and envision it fully furnished and you enjoying it. Take the time to make it yours. This exercise helps focus your reticular activating system. If you want to make a dream a reality, act as if it's already true.

Draw a pictogram of all of your dreams. Meditate on them, and get your family involved also. If you want a car, get a picture of it. Don't forget to get a picture of the house you visited. Find pictures that reflect what you want to achieve as a person, as a couple, and as an entrepreneur. Write the date on it, and print many copies of it. Stick them in visible areas like your car, bathroom, night table, office, cubicle, and your screen saver. Look at the pictogram every day, and ask yourself, "What am I doing today to reach my dreams?"

With your pictogram in key places, I want you to apply a simple filter known as SMART for each one of your dreams. This is a well-known, goal-setting technique that's applicable to dreams as well. It stands for:

(S) Specific

(M) Measurable

(A) Achievable

(R) Relevant/Realistic

(T) Time

Go over your dream again and see if it's specific, measurable, achievable, relevant and realistic for you. Make sure you've specified an amount of time in which to achieve it. Do you have an accountability system set up to measure your progress? If you can't answer yes to all these questions, then you need to find the tools to do so.

The key to reaching your dream and executing the plans we've defined is found in the word "accountability." Are you accountable to someone about your dreams? Do you have someone to share your progress, your shortcomings, and your current state with? Through the many strategic plans I've helped design, I've noticed how many organizations tend to overlook this vital element. Your goals cannot be reached without including it in the process.

Why is it so important to be specific and accountable? One example can share great insight into this. Do you know what the number one goal in the world is? The most common New Year's resolution is not happiness or money, but weight loss. Yet what's the number one health concern worldwide? Obesity. This shows that there is a gross inconsistency at a global level, as well as an enormous gap in its execution. When you say, "I want to lose weight," you're really not specific enough, nor do you have any way of being held accountable for it. But if you say, "By March 15th, 2018, I will lose 30 pounds and have 21% body fat, and I'm going to work out at the gym and schedule my weekly progress with a nutritionist," you're bound to get better results.

This is another key element to reaching your dreams: they must be specific, measurable, achievable, and relevant, within a specific time frame and have an accountability system set up for it.

The 2P + T = P Model (purpose, passion, talent, and profitability)

If you don't make your dreams a reality,
reality will snatch them away from you.
– Eric Pio

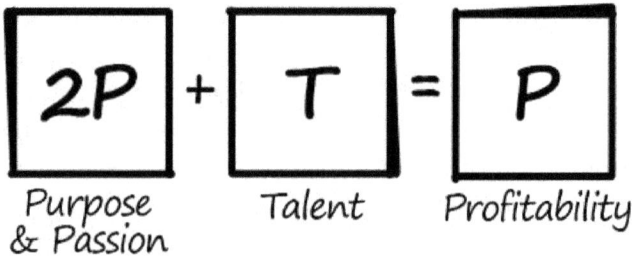

$$2P + T = P$$

Purpose & Passion   Talent   Profitability

Every great business undertaking is a result of a great entrepreneur. Many researchers have asked themselves, "What makes a business successful? What makes a person successful?" Let's go over the tools that will help you answer these questions.

One of the most consistent contemporary writers to address this challenge is Jim Collins, author of *Good to Great*. This book reveals the findings of his research in a number of corporations that have yielded the greatest returns throughout a 15-year period. Collins discovered that these businesses have a combination of three key elements: something that moves them or for which they have a passion, something for which they have a unique talent, and mechanisms to measure their profitability.

Well-known professor at Claremont Graduate School and author of *Flow: The Psychology of Optimal Experience*, Mihaly Csikszentmihalyi describes the principle behind combining passion with talent. It's that delicate state of flowing that a trumpet player finds himself in at the pinnacle of his jazz performance that helps us better understand the state of high performance in an individual as well. It's highly unlikely to be successful without fusing these two elements together.

Sir Ken Robinson concurs with this. In his book *The Element* he analyzes how various people have discovered what makes them feel alive after fusing what they have a passion for with their talents and then cultivating that equilibrium on a daily basis.

Upon discovering these components, I considered that purpose was the leadership ingredient that marked the difference between someone ordinary and someone extraordinary. If you study any leader that has been a world changer, you'll discover that they had a clear purpose and an inner call that moved them. This is the reason why purpose is such a vital element. In fact, my studies on leadership at the Aspen Institute caused me to question altogether the use of the term "success" and to then replace it with "significance" or "transcendence." Indeed, it would be a good idea to take into account that our level of success can actually be measured in terms of our level of transcendence in life.

If you really wish to be successful in any venture, if you wish to transcend in business or in life, make sure you keep in mind the 2P + T=P Model: Purpose, Passion, Talent and Profitability.

Purpose: What am I here for? What is my calling?
Passion: What do I have a passion for? What really makes me happy?
Talent: What am I good at? What are my main strengths?
Profitability: How could I make this business profitable?

Let's look at each one in greater detail.

Purpose

*Someone once defined genius as the intensity of a purpose,
the ability to perform, and the patience to wait. Put all these together
and you end up with success.*
– Leo Muir

If I were to ask you right now, why are you here, what would your answer be? There's no doubt that this is a question we'll spend our entire lifetime discovering and perhaps we'll never arrive at a simple answer. In spite of this, little by little, through diverse events and experiences in life, you start getting an idea of what your contribution to this world could be and what path in life is best suited for you.

Usually when I hold a session on strategic planning, I reference a statement from Lewis Carroll's celebrated fairy tale *Alice in Wonderland*. When Alice comes to a crossroad and doesn't know which way to go, she asks the Cheshire Cat, "Would you tell me, please, which way I ought to go from here?"

"That depends a good deal on where you want to get to," the Cheshire Cat said.

"I don't much care where," Alice continues.

"Then anywhere will take you there," the cat wisely replies.

How will you ever know what path to take if you don't know what your purpose and goal in life are? That's why it's so important to meditate on these things.

*"Arriving at a crossing with four trails before him, he imagined the
crossroads where knights from long ago would mull which road to take.
Seeking to mimic them, quiet he stood for a time and having pondered
it well, released he the leashes of his faithful steed, leaving it up to it to
choose and following its first choice straight into a stable."*
– Don Quijote de la Mancha by Miguel Cervantes

Now what are you going to do? Will you take any route not knowing where you want to go, or will you simply go back to where you were—that safe place where you don't need to know your purpose in life?

If your purpose isn't clear, your decision-making process will be faulty. But if you have a clear purpose in life, you'll know what career to follow, what job offer to accept, what skills to develop, and what path to take in life. If you study the greatest leaders of mankind, you'll find even at a young age, a clear purpose in each one of their lives. Take, for example, Jesus Christ. Even while still a child, He knew what His calling was. That conviction led Him, even as a young boy, to study with the teachers of the law. It also provoked Him into making statements such as, "It's not my time yet" and to choose the right moment to start his ministry.

Peter Diamandis knew full well that he loved space, and he dedicated his life to it. Paul McCartney loved music, and he cultivated that calling. The Wright brothers envisioned a flying contraption that would transform the world. Our purpose might not be clearly laid out yet, but something we do know is what we have a passion for. If we join this to our talents, we will surely find inescapable clues to our calling and the things we need to experiment with to fine tune it.

Success isn't a matter of chance, and the sooner you think deeply on your purpose, the faster you'll equip yourself to attain it. A word of caution: Discovering your purpose takes time. You need to carefully meditate on it and validate it. To help you in this process, here are 14 self-analysis questions. Go through them slowly, thinking through each reply. Upon completion, you'll find some pointers to guide you through this reflection.

1. What naturally awakens your curiosity? This speaks mainly of your interests. In order to better answer this question, think of what non-fiction books you like to read. What documentaries do you like to watch? What headlines or articles do you like to read in newspapers and magazines? What do you like to learn more about?

2. What would you like to change in this world? This is a powerful question. What challenges in society irritate you? What news reports upset you the most? What would you like to change in the world to make it a better place?

3. What would you like to do or fulfill before you die? Make the list as extensive as possible.

4. What would you do if you knew that failure wasn't an option? Let's say there were no limitations and you were guaranteed success. To what would you dedicate your life?

5. What would you do if money weren't a factor? Sometimes we set barriers because of financial limitations. If they weren't there, what would you do?

6. What would you like people to say at your funeral? Imagine the funeral service with your closest loved ones. One by one, their turn comes up to speak. What would you like them to say about you? What kind of friend, colleague, or relative were you? What contributions or achievements would you like them to recall? What difference would you like to have made in their lives?

7. What activities do you enjoy? What activities make time fly by with you? Please include work and pastimes.

8. What tasks or assignments do you feel empower you? Think about the jobs you've had, the schools you've attended, or any volunteer work you've done. What activity in the past has made you feel fulfilled, productive, and wanting to do more of it?

9. What would you like people to know you for? What achievements are you proud of?

10. If you only had one wish in life, what would it be?

11. Whose life would you like to live? Which people (in the present or past) do you look up to the most? Who do you admire or perhaps even envy?

12. Which ideas inspire you the most? Why? These ideas can be about your life, career, society, or any other aspect. Examples of these might be free education for all, a safer world, etc.

13. Who would you like to spend more time with or be in relationship with? What types of people do you like to surround yourself with concerning lifestyles, occupations, wealth, or interests?

14. Do you take responsibility for what happens to you? Do you believe your decisions are to blame for the state you're in? Can you build your own future?

Go over each answer with the explanations below:

1. What are you naturally curious about? Your answer to this question says a lot about the subjects you have a passion for. Your answers offer insight into the type of profession or field in which you can develop.

2. What would you like to change in the world? To a certain degree, that which upsets you the most shows what really matters to you, what's closest to your heart. What you don't have a passion for will normally not move you.

3. What would you like to do before you die? The things you list not only shed light into your goals, but into your values as well. It reveals what's important to you and the type of lifestyle you would like to have.

4. What would you do if failure weren't an option? This question helps you think free of limitations. You most likely wrote things you enjoy doing.

5. What would you do if finances weren't a limitation? The answers to this question will help you remove obstacles in your manner of thinking, piercing into your deepest desires. Bear in mind that you can make money doing what you have a passion for.

6. What would you like to hear at your funeral? Your answer to this reflects what you mostly value in life, how you would like to live that life, and what mostly matters to you.

7. What do you enjoy doing? It's very likely that your passion is found in one of these activities.

8. What tasks or activities have made you feel empowered? When you're passionate about a certain project or assignment, you feel energized, you get excited, and you don't tire so easily. When your natural talents and abilities come to life, you discover that you're a greater person than you imagined. The activities that make you feel good can help uncover your passion or at the very least draw you closer to discovering it.

9. What would you like to be known for in life? You can only feel proud of those things that matter to you. Obviously, you need to make sure that they really mean a great deal to you.

10. If you only had one wish in life, what would it be? Now that you've meditated on this, think of five people for whom you could help achieve their dream (including strangers). Afterward, identify the trends you pick up on. These may help draw you closer to your purpose.

11. Whose life would you like to live? Choose someone specific. The areas you admire in that person—their achievements, their lifestyle, or other aspects—will help shed light into your own.

12. What ideas inspire you the most? If there's an idea that really draws your interest, then that could be your purpose.

13. Who would you like to spend more time with or be in relationship with? The people around you will often influence you, causing you to imitate them. This helps highlight your interests and the trends you like to follow up on.

14. Do you assume responsibility for what happens to you? No one else can change your future and build the life you want. If you shift the responsibility to someone else, you'll be looking for answers in all the wrong places. If you answered yes to this one, then congratulations!

Now that you've completed these questions, read over your answers again. Do you see a pattern or trend? Try to identify those things you repeat in your answers; this will help you discover your passion and purpose in life. What did you find? What clues do you have about your purpose in life?

Passion

Don't worry about what the world needs. Ask yourself what makes
you feel alive and do it. What the world is mostly in need of
are people that feel alive at what they do.
– Howard Thurman

"I see you finished your story," Mom said upon stumbling on a note I had in a notebook where I used to spend hours writing.

"Yes, would you like to hear it tonight?" I asked. And so my dad took that fairy tale, *The Story of the Lost Dawn*, to a children's magazine (Revista Chicos) in Guatemala. It was the very first work I ever published. I was nine years old.

One year later, my parents as well as teachers from the Evelyn Rogers School I attended in Guatemala, invited me to participate in a national competition known as Mayor for a Day. I dubiously complied. "What if I don't win?" I asked my parents every day.

"Whether or not you participate is up to you, but if you don't, you'll always have the doubt of whether or not you could have done it." They knew me all too well, I couldn't handle the realm of doubt, so I accepted.

In one of the final interviews, I remember them asking, "Are you Red or Cream?" referring to my team of choice from the National Soccer League. The Municipality of Guatemala sponsored the municipal team—the Reds.

"Well, I don't really follow soccer that much, but at home everyone's a Cream," I said, my face blushing.

"We appreciate your honesty," he said with a smile.

After leaving the interview, my dad asked with excitement, "How did it go?"

"Great, I won," came my assured reply.

"The important thing is that you gave it a shot. No matter what happens, you're a winner" he said as he joined in our expectations.

"You'll see. I won. I'm sure of it." And sure enough, a few days later came the call confirming my convictions. I had won.

I was named Mayor for a Day in Guatemala City. The week prior to my appointment was nothing short of magical. In preparation for having me "take possession," I was able to speak with the State cabinet and the president of the nation at that time, Vinicio Cerezo.

On November 30, 1990, I was handed the Edilicia Staff, a symbolic wand given to the current mayor in office. I remember it like it was only yesterday. The first thing I did was find how to get a street paved. *Mayors pave streets, right?* I reasoned.

The street I lived on back then led to Francisco Marroquin University, one of the most important universities in my country and to a bathhouse, which today houses another important institute of higher learning, Galileo College. I started talking to my staff on the radio they assigned me, asking them to inspect the street. "I've only got one day to get it approved, so I really need your help," I urged.

Can you imagine the joy and the importance a ten-year-old felt to see the street getting paved the following week? Even to this day, whenever I teach graduate courses at either university, I drive down that same street with the thought, *It can be done!*

That's how my desire for entrepreneurship was birthed. I remember thinking to myself, "There really is nothing that can't be done, regardless of the age or context you live in. If you really want to change something, you've got to do something about it."

You see things; and you say "Why?"
But I dream things that never were; and I say "Why not?"
– George Bernard Shaw

Your purpose is intricately linked to your passion. If you still haven't discovered your purpose, the things you're passionate about could help provide clues to unveiling it. Our passions are those things that consume us with palpable emotions. The word is derived from the Latin *passio*, which means suffering.

What would you like to change in the world? The majority of entrepreneurs suffer in order to change something that in their eyes can make the world a better place. Perhaps the product doesn't exist yet, or the company that has it doesn't offer quality service for it. That healthy type of suffering, per se, is usually what drives us toward a new venture or undertaking.

Why is passion so vital for sustainable success? Co-authors Jerry Porras, Steward Emery, and Mark Thompson of *Success Built to Last*, interviewed over 400 successful people over a 10-year period. Their work showed how loving what one does is a vital condition for long-term success.

According to the authors, "Much has been said about the importance of loving what one does, but most people simple don't buy that idea. Sure, it would be great to love what you do, but for practical effects, most people can't afford to. Now, here's the bad news—it's dangerous not to love what you do. The hard truth is that unless you love what you do, you'll always lose out to someone who does. For every person that doesn't love their job or the relationship they're in, there's going to be someone that loves it. And this person is going to be willing to work harder and longer for what they know they'll earn and gain as years go by."

Multi-million-dollar investor Warren Buffet said on one occasion, "There is a difference between me and you, and it's simply that I wake up every morning with the opportunity of doing what I love to do every day. If you really want to learn something from me, then this is the best advice I can give you."

Author Curt Rosengren wrote that bringing passion to what one does every day is "ridiculously easy," seeing that it emanates from simple authenticity. He defines passion as, "the energy that comes from bringing more of you into what you do." Passion literally becomes an extension of who you are.

Over 2000 years ago, Aristotle wrote that true happiness is founded in self-realization within the broader mankind, acquired via the exercise of virtue. Generally speaking, a virtue can be defined as, "the added excellence to something such as perfection, the goodwill for the fulfillment, or perfect realization of a natural inclination." In his work, the *Nicomachean Ethics*, Aristotle claims that human virtue isn't a skill or a passion but a habit. To claim that it is a habit means that it is a result of a teaching and not by nature, that it manifests through continual practice or repetition. In short, Aristotle invites us to perfect our talents for it is the only means by which we may achieve happiness.

On the other hand, we also need to understand that simply doing what one loves won't automatically bring happiness, meaning, or fulfillment to one's life. Even with all of our passion, we still have desires that are in conflict with each other, such as the tension between our job and our home. The key is found in being aware of our needs, our passions, and other dimensions for a full, holistic life-style: work, family, health, happiness, and community. Live in such a way that each element receives their due attention balanced with the importance of proper rest. Now it's your turn to define your passion.

"Sometimes life strikes you in the head with a brick. Don't lose faith. I'm fully convinced that the only thing that kept me going was that I loved what I did. You need to find what you really love. And that is as true for your work as it is for your lovers. Your work is going to fill a large and important part of your life, and the only way to truly be satisfied is by doing what you consider is great work. And the only way to do great work is to love what you do. If you haven't found it yet, keep looking. Don't settle. As with all the matters of the heart, you'll know when you find it. And just like any great relationship, it gets better and better as the years roll on. So keep looking until you find it. Don't settle."
—*Steve Jobs commencement speech at Stanford*

What is your passion? What do you love doing? If you could do anything in life, what would it be?

Talent

"Talent isn't a heavenly gift, but the fruit of systematic development of special qualities."
— *Jose Maria Rodero*

"Everyone believes that talent is a matter of luck, but no one ever believes that luck might be a matter of talent."
— *Jacinto Benavente*

Have you ever thought what your "unfair competitive advantage" is? I like to add the word "unfair" because something that you're good at might seem exactly that to others. In what has God made you more talented? If you've ever been told, "No one's quite the storyteller that you are," "Learning is so easy with you," "I just love the way you draw" or any other statement like this that highlights a certain talent, pay attention to it, and write it down. True talent is always followed by confirmation.

Your talent is your dominant strength, that which you can do more easily than others: negotiate, establish relationships, draw, teach, solve calculations, analyze problems, find creative solutions, cook, consult, sculpt, hear—we all have talents, yet we don't all put them to good use. It's common to hear, "You've got these weaknesses, please work on them." But it's rare to hear, "You've got these strengths, develop them even more." Sir Ken Robinson likens talents to precious stones that can remain buried forever if you don't discover them and polish them.

Now we'll focus on discovering your talents. For this, you will need to answer some questionnaires and complete some exercises that will allow us to reach certain important conclusions. You must be as honest as possible. Remember, there are no good or bad talents, just those in disuse for positive purposes.

The first thing you'll do is answer this survey, a self-assessment. Make a list of the talents that you think you have. You'll then ask five or more people that know you in different contexts (family, work, friend, social) what they think your talents or abilities are. Here's an example you can use in your notebook. Don't focus on evaluating them yet, simply jot down every strength that comes to mind.

> Person #1:
> Where do I know them from:
> What talent do they recognize in me?
>
> Person #2:
> Where do I know them from:
> What talent do they recognize in me?
>
> Person #3:
> Where do I know them from:
> What talent do they recognize in me?

Are the talents and abilities you listed similar to the ones your friends stated? Analyze why they are similar or why they vary.

Now we are going to take the Herrmann Test used in the *The Whole Brain Business Book*. Remember that no test can classify you under a certain category since we are constantly evolving and developing. However, this test will help give you an idea of your predominant behaviors.

The herrmann test

Below are 10 rows with 4 words each. Choose a word from each row that mostly describes you and write a 4 next to it. Write a 3 next to the word that second most describes you, and so on. Afterward, add up the points in each column and circle the highest amounts.

cold	disciplined	sympathetic	passionate
skeptical	punctual	extroverted	indecisive
perfect	stubborn	disorganized	emotional
correct	organized	pioneer	expressive
formal	careful	dreamer	flexible
blunt	verifier	spontaneous	tolerant
aggressive	hard	original	sensitive
results-oriented	insurer	inspiring	sentimental
audacious	systematic	intuitive	amiable
objective	controlling	sociable	affectionate
Total	Total	Total	Total
Blue Analytical	**Green Organized**	**Yellow Visualizer**	**Red Personalized**

The columns with your highest scores represent your dominant color. Let's see to what application each color refers.

BLUE	YELLOW
Analytical	Visualizer
Logical and critical thinking of events	Imaginative by nature, thinks globally, speculates
Number processing and measuring	Impetuous, doesn't go by the rules, loves surprises
Rational and realistic, knows how things work	Curious and integrative, experiments, and takes risks

GREEN	RED
Organized	Personalized
Plans ways of doing things, organizes events, reviews carefully	Interpersonal, intuitive, and expressive
Prudent, sets procedures and sequences, is pro-active, makes things happen, dislikes ambiguity	Sensitive to surroundings, enjoys teaching, is emotional and kinesthetic, provokes teamwork

What can you deduce about yourself from each color?

Bear in mind that it pays to develop our strengths. Successful entrepreneurs align their strengths to their dominant personality, allowing them to engage in tasks that are appealing to them. What is your current job like? Is your personality profile compatible with your current job description? The following table can help you identify your styles and dominant preferences as well as the ones of those around you. What does your spouse enjoy doing, your children, your work team?

BLUE	YELLOW
Analytical	Visualizer
Enjoys:	Enjoys:
• Working alone	• Taking risks
• Applying formulas	• Inventing solutions
• Analyzing data	• Vision-casting
• Making things work right	• Promoting changes
• Solving difficult problems	• Experimenting
• Logical processing	• Creating new things
• Challenges	• Designing
• Explaining things	• Selling things
	• Variety of options
GREEN	RED
Organized	Personalized
Enjoys:	Enjoys:
• Building things	• Making teams work well
• Being in control	• Expressing ideas
• Organized surroundings	• Creating relationships
• Preserving the status quo	• Teaching/training
• Paperwork tasks	• Listening and speaking to others
• Planning things	• Working with people
• Stabilizing things	• Communication skills
• Meeting deadlines	• Helping others
• Structured tasks	• Expressing feelings
• Tending to details	• Giving advice/counseling
• Administrating	• Being part of a team

According to what you've analyzed on your personality profile, what are your major strengths? What activities could you perform to maximize those strengths? Do you want to undertake a business venture? List 25 business ideas that could maximize your preferences.

I once met an entrepreneur who after going over these principles said, "I've got it! What I love in life is music, so then I should focus on singing."

"Good, I'd like to hear you sing," I replied. The moment he started singing, people around me started making faces of uneasiness, grief, fright, and even horror. "So what other talents do you have?" I continued.

His face just lit up, "I love to organize things. I'm great at keeping a track of things and scheduling. I'm actually quite meticulous."

"In the music world, how do you think you could use that talent?" I said.

"That's easy. Singers tend to be very disorganized with their agendas and personal finances."

"So what do you think you could do?" Today, that entrepreneur is the agent of a number of recording artists and according to emails we've exchanged, he's delighted about being able to mix his passion with his talent.

Profitability

> *Doing what is strategically correct is more important than doing what*
> *is immediately profitable.*
> *– Philip Kotler*

How can I make my undertaking profitable? The way to live off my purpose, my passion, and my talent requires one more vital piece of knowledge. It's common for certain highly competitive industries to have a clear purpose, passion, and talent, yet lack a clear way of making it profitable. If you lack financial training, allow me to submit the following equation, summarizing your financial needs, to better understand your business.

P = R - E
Profit = Revenue - Expenses

Upon closer analysis, companies have two options to maximize earnings, either increase their revenue or reduce their expenses. Non-profit organizations have the same challenges, except for the distribution of earnings.

In order to make a business undertaking profitable, it's pivotal to decide how to bill customers, collect payments, and create revenue. You can set product and service pricing following the same model as your competition, or you can opt for innovative strategies. In the book, *Blue Ocean Strategy*, authors W. Chan Kim and Renee Mauborgne researched how different companies changed their billing practices from a traditional approach to one better fitted to meeting customers' needs. Did you know Blockbuster was the first company to come out with movie rentals? Prior to that, you only had the option of buying movies. And today we've witnessed first-hand how this model has been taken over by Netflix's popular subscription system and access to unlimited amounts of movies.

In 1997, Reed Hastings was facing a $40 bill for not returning an *Apollo 13* DVD back to Blockbuster on time. The amount seemed exorbitant, and he refused to pay it. That's when Hastings decided to create a business that would do away with late fees and simply charge a monthly subscription for an unlimited amount of movie rentals. And that's how Netflix was birthed—and it also began the demise of Blockbuster.

Let's look at a few examples to glean ideas on how to charge for the products and services your business has to offer.

Some key questions to consider are the following: How do I make my venture profitable? How do I guarantee revenue? How do I minimize expenses?

In order to introduce you to these concepts, please go over the following:

Business	How do they bill they're customers?	What about the competition?
Uber	20% for those providing the service.	Normal taxis, 80% for those providing the service.
Amazon	15% royalties for digital books published on Kindle.	Publishing houses, 50–80% for its authors.
Facebook Ads	Cost per action (resulting from advertising)	Traditional advertising, charge for activities carried out.

Today's modern day businesses are transforming the way they bill their customers and increase revenue. Google offers many of its services for free, but it sells advertising. Facebook went from being a guide to help locate friends to an advertising and social interacting platform for businesses. Angry Birds offers a "freemium" strategy where a part of the product is free, but there are charges for additional upgrades and applications within the game. Organizations such as TED offer their knowledge for free, but they use a number of crowdfunding tools to continue to grow. And finally, businesses such as Pebble, Coolest Cooler, Exploding Kittens, Ouya, Pono Music, The Veronica Mars Movie Project, Reading Rainbow, Torment: Tides of Numenera, and Project Eternity raised millions of dollars through the Kickstarter platform. High-impact, social undertakings can be started on platforms such as Hero X in which talent and funding can be found via contests and competitions. Procuring finances really isn't an obstacle to starting a venture and realizing your dream.

Taking into account your purpose, passion, and talent—what problem can you solve? What need can you meet?

In order to meet this need or solve this problem, make a list of the products or services you are able to offer. What are ways to gain revenue from these products or services? What costs or expenses would you have to incur when offering these products or services? Write your answers in your notebook.

I, the Entrepreneur

True glory has a root system and expands; vain pretensions
fall to the ground and wither away.
– Marco Tulio Ciceron

Up until this point, we've been talking about you, your purpose, your passion, and your talent. We've also done a brief review of the products and services you can offer and how to bill them. Despite the fact that this book is about entrepreneurs and business undertakings, we have yet to clearly define the concept.

Let's look at a definition:

Entrepreneurship is the process of creating a new entity with an added value, allotting the necessary time and effort, and embracing the social and monetary risks, while in turn receiving financial rewards, personal freedom, and satisfaction from it.

(Hisrich, Robert; Peters, Michael; Shepherd, Dean. Entrepreneurship. McGraw-Hill press. 7th. Edition 2009.)

This definition highlights four basic aspects of being an entrepreneur:

First, entrepreneurship involves the process of creation. This new entity has to be of value to the entrepreneur as well as to the potential user.

Second, the venture requires time and effort.

Third, it involves rewards, independence, and a sense of personal satisfaction. When talking about for-profit entrepreneurs, the financial rewards play a large role in the process.

The final aspect encompasses taking on the venture's necessary risks since the future is uncertain. Nonetheless, the level of uncertainty can be managed through research of the business to be developed.

Worldwide statistics from diverse sources demonstrate that the desire to start a business has been inherent in people's attitudes since the end of the millennia. If you are reading this book, it's because you are part of these statistics and desire to start a business yourself. Although being an entrepreneur is an aspirational desire; not everyone is willing to take on the risks that come with it.

While interviewing Guatemalan businesses and businesspeople for my book, I was surprised to discover that Walter de la Cruz, founder of Cafe Barista, owned a business that had gone under prior to opening his widely successful chain of coffee shops. Today, he has partnered with one of the most important business groups of Latin America, Multi Inversiones.

I found that in the 1970s, Miss Yolanda Cofiño tried to sell her first McDonald's restaurant, yet no one wanted to purchase it. Everyone deemed it had no future. Afterward, she invented the Happy Meal as well as a number of other innovations that are now known worldwide.

I also found that the Paiz family spent a number of years educating the consumer in the concept of the Despensa Familiar (low-cost convenience store), for it wasn't readily understood. Today, it's a brand that forms part of Walmart's business model in a number of countries.

People many times ask me, "Do you know of any investors that might be interested in supporting me?" However, upon inquiring what they are willing to risk and put on the line, many have replied, "Well, I'm providing the idea," or "I'm not about to leave my job, but I do hope to get the necessary capital I need." If you really wish to undertake a business venture, you must examine yourself on some very sensitive matters. Here are a few questions that can help explore your focus even further. No one will ever be willing to invest in an idea that you're not fully convinced about.

- Have I really created something that will add value to potential users?
- Am I willing to invest time into this creation?
- Am I willing to work harder than ever before on it?
- Am I willing to lose money on it?
- Am I willing to lose time on it?
- Is my family willing to let me dedicate my time to this venture?
- Am I willing to make less than I'm currently making?
- Am I willing to work more hours than I currently am?
- Am I willing to sacrifice my own personal time for it?
- Am I willing to go through high levels of variability in my expenses?
- Am I willing to quit my job for this idea?
- Am I willing to take on debts for this idea?
- Am I willing to sell my belongings for this idea?
- Am I willing to minimize my budget for this idea?

If you've really been honest with yourself and you feel that you're still not ready, it could be because of three reasons. The first reason is that what you want to do really is not your calling or passion, or you don't have the talent to carry it out. Another reason is that you haven't figured out how to make it profitable yet. And the final reason is that it's not the right time, and you need to get better equipped for it.

On the other hand, if these questions have motivated you even more and you've already defined some preliminary ideas on what you want to do, use the following diagram to prioritize them and your undertakings to get the maximum impact in life.

Where would you open up your business?

Viability: How feasible is it to start that business or project in the short term?

Impact: What solid results will the business or project yield in the short run?

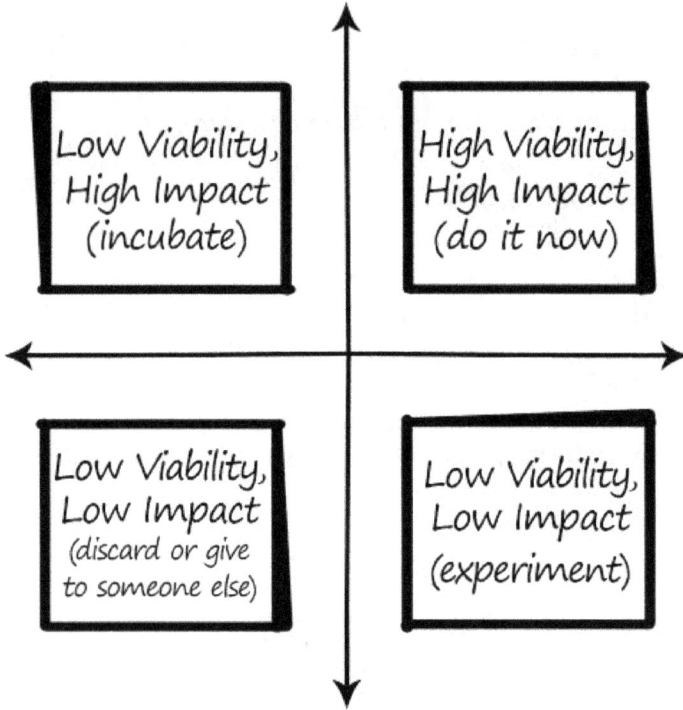

If you placed your startup in the upper left-hand box, you probably need to give it more time in the planning stage, or you may be missing all of the necessary elements to make it a success.

If you placed your startup in the lower left-hand box, it might not be the right venture for you. Remember, the key is focus.

If you placed your startup in the lower right-hand box, it's the perfect opportunity to launch and learn (a lean startup). This venture might not be exactly what you had in mind for the long run, but you can gain valuable experience as an entrepreneur from it.

If you placed your startup in the upper right-hand box, then you're in the best position possible. It's an undertaking you could launch in the short run with important results for your life. A vital key here is to confirm with other people that your startup really is located here.

Ready to get started?

According to many different entrepreneurs that I've interviewed and studied throughout the years, do you know what the secret to success is? Allow me to answer this with a simple story. Three frogs were sitting on a large leaf in a swamp. One of them decides to jump off. How many are left? You might have thought two because one decided to jump. You might have thought none because once the first one jumped, it startled the others and they followed. Both of these answers are wrong. How many were left? Three. You see, one of them decided to jump off, but never did. The key, as we are seeing throughout the book, is found in execution. To the degree that you make decisions and roll up your sleeves and actually do it, you'll be successful—I assure you. If you've made up your mind to launch your startup, let's see how the big ones do it.

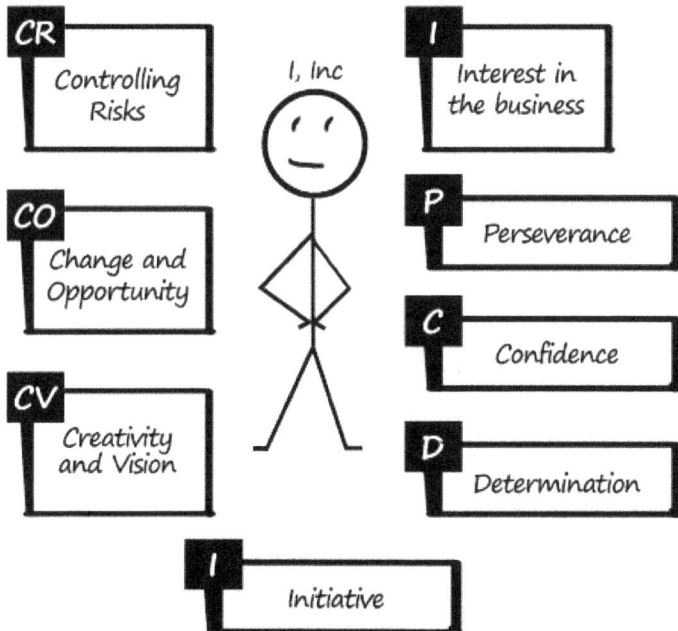

Attributes of successful entrepreneurs

Motivation gets you started, but habit keeps you going.
— Jim Rohn

Monopoly (1935)

Charles Darrow, an unemployed engineer, designed a game in which players would compete for great wealth and total dominion of a city's real estate. He probably never imagined how his creation—Monopoly—would become the highest selling board game in history. His concept, nevertheless, wasn't entirely original. It could have easily been an adaptation of the Landlord's Game, patented in 1924 by Elizabeth Maggie, which was also based on the sales and rental of railroad lines. Darrow created the banker's image, which is a key feature in the game. He named the properties after the streets of Atlantic City and got his own patent in 1935. Charles first tried to sell his idea to Parker Brothers, but they turned him down citing 52 design flaws. Nonetheless, Darrow didn't give up and sold 5,000 handmade sets in a department store in Philadelphia. Parker Brothers quickly had a change of heart.

Chocolate chip cookies (1933)

In 1933, Ruth Wakefield, manager of a small hotel known as Toll House in Whitman, Massachusetts, invented one of the most popular foods known to man. Her recipe for making butter cookies required chocolate to bake them, which she didn't have at the moment. So in its place she chopped a chocolate bar into pieces, thinking it would melt in the cookie. Nestle was so impressed with the cookie's success that they cut a deal with Miss Ruth: a life-long supply of chocolate in exchange for the recipe. She accepted, and the instructions for making Toll House chocolate chip cookies are still printed on the bag to this day.

Car radio (1930)

When Henry Ford's first Model T rolled off the assembly line, music in a car meant the passengers had to sing away. Nonetheless, two brothers, Paul and Joseph Galvin, founders of Chicago Galvin Manufacturing, makers of electric converters for battery-operated radios, were looking for other sources of income following the economic downfall. Partnering with William Lear, owner of a radio parts shop in the same building, and Elmer Wavering, another engineer, they installed the first car radio on May 1930 in a Studebaker. The following month, Paul drove 800 miles to a radio manufacturer's trade show in Atlantic City, New Jersey. Lacking a space or booth at the convention, he parked near the event and raised the volume to his invention drawing the attention of many onlookers in attendance. In 1933, orders started coming in, including from Ford himself who started offering pre-installed radios right from the factory. Shortly thereafter, Galvin Manufacturing changed their name to Motorola.

I've specifically selected business ventures from the 1930s, right when the United States was undergoing the Great Depression. Crisis or opportunity? Remember how we mentioned that entrepreneurs don't demonstrate any specific psychological traits, but what they do exhibit are clearly defined behaviors. In other words, consistent habits.

Someone once defined being a businessperson as someone who takes creative human actions and builds something of value out of virtually nothing. It is the relentless search for opportunity, independent of the available resources or lack thereof. It requires vision, passion, and commitment to lead others in the pursuit of that vision. It also requires the willingness to take calculated risks."

Our current educational system doesn't stimulate the development of an entrepreneurial spirit. In fact, it actually teaches conformity and a codependent work culture. Children's creative skills are not taken into account despite them being a key foundational component in most business people.

What attributes are evident in some of the greatest entrepreneurs?

Interest in the business itself. A businessman must have more than a mere casual attitude for the business because he will need to overcome many obstacles and problems. Unless he has a passion or purpose driving him, the business will not be successful. That personal and emotional commitment must be reflected in the tenaciousness for bringing his ideas to fruition.

Perseverance in spite of failure. Failure must be embraced as a learning experience. Obstacles and problems to overcome are permanent tests for which you must display persistence and not give in. Many business people attain success only after failing a number of times. You must set goals that are in proportion to your knowledge and capacity. It's not about reaching the ideal but about achieving acceptable results. It's been said that "business people never fail, they just go through learning experiences." Prior to being successful, Walt Disney and Henry Ford failed a number of times.

Self-confidence. You must choose an activity that allows you to express yourself creatively as well as facilitate your personal and professional development. Never underestimate your skills and capacities. Businesspeople trust in their abilities and in the business concept itself. They believe they have the ability to do anything they set their mind to. That trust is commonly founded on an in-depth knowledge of the target market or industry, having taken months or even years of intense research to acquire. You must endeavor to know as much as possible about the activity you've chosen and continue to stay updated in it. Many times this knowledge can turn you into an expert coupled with the advantages it encompasses.

Self-determination. Self-motivation and self-determination are paramount elements for success. Business people act by self-will and never deem themselves victims of fate. They are convinced that failure or success is in their hands. Those who believe that success is a matter of luck, the economy, or other external factors will probably never make it as a businessperson.

Risk management. It's common to think that business people love living life on the edge. This isn't so. They normally try to minimize risks and turn to their own experience or professional assessment before making any important decisions. They're also constantly assessing the opportunity of turning ideas into real-life applications. Many people gain experience working for other companies prior to starting their own business, allowing them to reduce the amount of risk they need to take. They don't invest all of their time and resources into the business until it starts looking feasible. Risk taking is a business attribute, otherwise it would be impossible to apply ideas and transform them into reality. Notwithstanding, the risks referred to here are calculated risks that many times one engages in more strenuously at the beginning stages of a venture and are sought to be reduced as soon as possible.

Changes and opportunities. Businesspeople are gifted with the ability to find and measure business opportunities, collect the necessary resources to make the most of them, and perform accordingly to reach success. For most people, change is something terrifying, to be avoided at all costs, but that is not the case with entrepreneurs. To them, change is the norm. They seek it out, respond to it, and use it as an opportunity. This adjustment to change forms the basis of innovation.

Creativity and overview. Imagination is one of the distinctive attributes found in business people and one of the reasons why they are so successful in the business world. They have a keen ability to pick up on opportunities that other people overlook. They also perceive the different scenarios and alternate circumstances that may happen. It's common for entrepreneurs to view things in a holistic way. They have the ability to see the big picture, while others only see the parts. There is a process of market reconnaissance that's based on picking up on the available information, allowing them to see the whole atmosphere of the business as well as envision the overview of the activity they are to develop. This also helps to shed light on the competitive arena in which they'll engage.

Initiative and refinement. Another distinguishing attribute found in successful businesspeople is the drive and energy they have to act on, bringing their ideas to practical everyday life. Many people have good ideas, but if these don't turn into action, it will be impossible to achieve their purpose. A good businessperson also demands quality and efficiency. They strive to do things better, faster, and more effectively. Business people always seek to reach and exceed quality standards.

Motivation. Businessmen aren't only driven by the desire to make money; there are other motivational factors that play a role just as important as profit. Some of the most relevant ones are: perform an activity allowing you to use your talents and personal abilities, manage your time with greater independence in life, build something for the family, find satisfaction when facing risks and challenges, live in a certain place, and enjoy a certain type of lifestyle, among others. In short, a mindset of growth and abundance toward life.

Assessing my traits as an entrepreneur

Answer the following questions in your notebook:

- How do I feel?
- Am I ready to start a business?
- What must I consider prior to undertaking a business venture?
- Do I really have a clear passion for the business I wish to start up?
- Will I be persistent even if I fail at first?
- Do I trust in my entrepreneurial abilities?
- Am I self-motivated?
- Do I view change as an opportunity?
- Am I creative?
- Do I keep my word?
- Do I have a genuine motivation for starting my business?

Business Idea Generator

*Truly creative people are driven by the desire to reach a goal
and not by the desire to defeat everyone else.*
– Ayn Rand

By now, you've probably already made up your mind to be an entrepreneur. The next two questions you need to answer are: Do you have a business idea? Have you identified an opportunity?

Did you know that...

IBM started off in the business of wiring and cables, and later expanded to watches? Their sales in the 1920s were a few million dollars. Their successful office computer followed by the personal computer didn't appear until many years later.

The Polaroid Corporation was founded on a product of light polarization to help prevent transit accidents caused by light glare from headlamps of oncoming traffic. The company then grew to an industry leader by employing the same technology on a different application: instant photographs.

The McDonalds Happy Meal was created in Guatemala after Yolanda de Cofiño observed how parents would buy meals for their children with much of it going to waste because of their large portions. Thus, the children's menu was invented, revolutionizing the fast-food industry worldwide.

The idea for Cafe Barista's coffee shop was birthed in 1993 during a visit of Mr. Walter de la Cruz to New Orleans. However, it wasn't until 2004 when the first coffee shop was officially opened. It took him 11 years to prepare and create the concept that went from an idea to a successful undertaking.

Where to find inspiration for business ideas?

Category	Where to get inspired?
Inventions: What's new?	HeroX Kickstarter United States Patent and Trademark Office
Hobbies or personal interests: What do I like to do in my free time?	Discoverahobby.com Notsoboringlife.com
Conferences, Conventions and Trade Shows: Where can I meet more people like me?	Associations related to your business undertaking Professional clubs
Search for new products or services not sold locally: What can I find in other markets that might work locally?	Alibaba.com Amazon.com Ebay.com
Trending topics in Google or Twitter: What's relevant in the world today?	Twitter.com Google Trends TweetDeck
Reading academic texts or trade magazines: What is the research trend about something?	Google Scholar Magazines.com
Travel is life: What experiences can I engage in that will allow me to see other realities?	TripAdvisor.com Alliance Abroad

What can I do?

Write down ideas you can use to search out new business opportunities.

Systematically observe changes around you. We are now safe to arrive at two important conclusions. The first one is that observation of changes in our business or our social and financial surroundings is paramount. It must be systematic, organized, and rigorous, based on objective data and validated via direct contact and not by intuition. The second conclusion is that a modest idea from social observations can easily become a better business opportunity than an apparently brilliant, technical invention. It's important to note that the first option, the modest idea, carries much less risk than the second one. Never forget that an entrepreneur takes on moderate risks and doesn't play russian roulette at business.

Upon completing this exercise of observing factors of social change, you'll quickly devise a list of possible business opportunities based on the new needs these changes produce.

Let's see a few of them:

Changes in personal income. A significant increase in the net income of a population or a segment of it in a developed society can easily cater to new needs such as those associated with personal care: gyms, dieting, clothing, hair salons, and plastic surgery clinics.

It can also generate changes in more comfortable amenities: heating, air conditioning, more modern appliances, decoration, renovation, sales or rentals of a second home, entertainment, lifestyles, restaurants, technology, and robotics.

Changes in educational levels. If we begin to observe a notable rise in a population's educational level, some new needs that might surface are professional development, languages, books, journals, magazines, online libraries, greater ecological and environmental awareness, such as creation of businesses catering to new and improved recycling processes or ecofriendly practices, greater sensitivity to urban housing, as well as activities related to building renovation.

Changes in leisure time. A third factor to be considered could be an increase in free time in a population, allowing for greater interest in hobbies and pastimes. New needs of the following nature could surface: sports centers and specialized stores; developmental creativity centers, such as schools for plastic and visual arts, cinematography, theater, domestic crafts, music, dance, shows, entertainment, travel; and gardening and landscaping, such as teaching, tools, plants, books, and nurseries.

Changes in life expectancy. In today's society, there has been a notable shift in a population's life expectancy. Medical attention and scientific breakthroughs have extended people's life spans. This in turn has given rise to new needs, such as specialized medical services for the elderly, geriatrics, nursing homes and private residential institutions, trips and recreation, creation of infrastructure and specialized services for the elderly.

Changes of women in the work force. Cultural and economical development in a country will reflect a notable increase in the percentage of women joining the work force. This trend can give way to a number of new needs, such as daycares, housekeeping, ready-made pre-cooked or frozen products, and new appliances, such as freezers, coolers, microwave ovens, etc. Also, there may be more magazines aimed at working women.

Changes in lifestyle: solitude. The number of people living by themselves is continually growing in urban societies. Whether it's due to marriage, separation, widowhood, or simply because of their professional careers, they all provide new opportunities for business ventures, such as furnished apartments, appliances for single people, new presentations and packaging in food commodities (frozen, ready-made soups, etc.) marriage agencies and contacts, and recreational activity centers, such as clubs, associations, and social gatherings.

Changes in a population's fears. Many fears or phobias arise in our society as well as greater emphasis made on those that already exist, such as war, theft, rape, air travel accidents, etc. These in turn produce new needs that facilitate the emergence of new enterprises, such as earthquake or nuclear shelters, bulletproof doors, personal security, parking facilities, buildings, storage areas, alarm systems, and new security methods or procedures.

Changes in labor markets. Societies that perceive a notable increase in unemployment face new challenges that generate new needs, such as professional re-certification schools for specific activities, possibilities in self-employment or delivery services, volunteer or non-profit work, and digital businesses such as Freelancer.com.

Changes in energy surroundings. An increasing lack of traditional energy resources gives way to new needs, such as alternate sources of energy, solar, thermal, wind, and methods for lowering energy consumption.

Changes in digital business. In the next few years, an estimated 3 billion people will enter the global digital market. This means an exponential increase in supply and demand. There's an infinite amount of new needs that the digital market can meet. Just think about how Amazon or Alibaba, both digital distributors, are in direct competition with Walmart. Also, notice how Amazon was a determining factor in Borders shutting down. You can also note how Barnes and Nobles is greatly reducing the amount of brick and mortar stores the bookstore chain owns.

Evaluating the business idea

What changes do you see all around you? Write them down. Once you identify a clear need or situation, you will have to identify a specific business opportunity, if in fact there is one. You must also assess your potential to meet it prior to crafting a detailed business plan. It's very common to identify and discard a number of ideas prior to adopting the ones most commercially viable for you. Below you will find a list of questions that will help you determine an opportunity and measure its potential business return.

- Is there a large enough market for it?
- Can I maintain costs low enough to make the business profitable?
- Is there room to grow?
- How strong is the competition?
- Do I possess the necessary skills/knowledge?

In addition, please complete the following phrases to develop a profile of your possible business undertaking. Remember to do these exercises in your notebook to keep a journal of your information.

- My current business idea is:
- The target market for this product or service is:
- How much could I sell it for?
- How much would it cost me to market it?
- What would be the expected profits?
- How much can I expect to grow?
- How will the competition react when I start my business?
- What's my capacity and knowledge to do it?
- Does this business fit within my purpose?
- Do I have a passion for this?
- Do I really have the talent to do it well?
- Can I make it profitable?

Now, before going on to more practical matters such as the business plan, allow me to share a very enriching story about entrepreneurship as a lifestyle.

The movie industry in Central America

"We believe that Carlos will never make it in college. We recommend he not go to school but just learn a trade." These were the words my school counselors used to sentence my future. My parents, nonetheless, believed in me. They always urged me to undertake any venture I desired.

Years later, I thought back on these words while giving a speech at the Organization of American States (OAS) in Geneva, Switzerland. What if I had listened to them? I surely wouldn't be where I am now, proudly representing Guatemala before the world as someone proving that it is possible to be successful, even with dyslexia. I'm now a strong advocate of technology as a teaching aid, promoting the CA Foundation's work, which dreams of changing the lives of those that learn in different ways.

My name is Carlos Arguello. My parents are Nicaraguan, but I was born in Guatemala with special needs. These needs helped mold my life. I had a problem with my eye movement, so I wasn't able to read well. I would get the letters confused and it was very frustrating that my teachers didn't know what was wrong with me. I was an active boy that enjoyed drawing, painting, and giving form to the thoughts in my mind.

I started off studying architecture. However, at the age of 17, I discovered that the teaching methodologies employed in Guatemala were distant from the vision that I carried within me. *What would I work in if I graduated?* was a thought that continually echoed in my mind. I didn't want to be an architect in the traditional sense, nor did I like graphic design. However, I loved technology, video games, and the arts. While meditating on the options available to me locally, I decided to embark on a journey that would transform my life forever.

Can't speak the language and penniless in America

Moving to the U.S. at the tender age of 17, without knowing English and not a dime in my pocket, was no easy feat. My aunt received me in her home, and it was the start of a new experience that quickly accelerated my growth, coupled with a solid assurance that hard work and dedication can help me achieve anything. And that's exactly what happened.

I knew that in order to work in the field that I loved, I had to study. In order to study, I needed money. So I started off in a job cleaning tables in Palo Alto, a city located near San Francisco. The kitchen wasn't my strong suit, and with a weak level of English, merely working there became quite a challenge. Notwithstanding, they gave me the opportunity to work as host in the restaurant. The pay wasn't too bad, but I knew that if I wanted to cover the costs of studying in the university with the best design program—the Academy of Arts—I had to move up to being a waiter because the tips would be better. I spent time practicing my English and training long hours to speak it, think it, and write it. Little by little, I started engaging with more customers and my self-confidence started to grow.

How to pay my way through college

The day finally arrived when I was accepted into the Academy of the Arts. I accomplished my main goal, but now I would have to work full-time as a waiter to cover my tuition—and that's exactly what I did for the next six years. The days were exhausting, but I never gave up, I set my eyes on the goal of one day graduating from university. I knew this was the ticket to new paths of opportunities for my dreams.

Six months prior to graduating, both my friend and I were offered an opportunity to work as interns at a technology firm. It was a competitive selection process, and though I would go eight months without a salary, I knew I would get the chance to work with $90,000 worth of equipment, not too mention the opportunity of growing in my professional and personal experience. To this day, I still wonder what it was that made them choose me. It must have been the enthusiasm I showed in my work; I was passionate about what I did.

Art Director at 23

At the age of 23, I was already working as an art director for the company, and we started winning international awards. I also started experimenting with digital paint, and though the industry was still in the beginning stages, my paintings were the first to come out. I had exhibitions of my work in France, Germany, and Japan.

I felt like I was at the apex of my career, celebrating the successes I shared with my team. Nonetheless, a crisis forced me to change paths and reassess the direction I was going in. The company went broke, and I was left without a job.

The crisis and the opportunity to start over again

That drastic change forced me to look for alternatives. I researched certain trends in the industry and envisioned the answer in entertainment and new digital technologies. I got involved in the production of Michael Jackson's "Black or White," scheduled to debut in November 1991. It was to be the first single on his recording known as *Dangerous*. I helped with a number of special effects, especially in the final sequence where we had to alter the faces of a number of people. It was an enormous privilege to work with such talented people that had also given life to the classic movie *Terminator*.

That experience opened a number of doors for me. On one opportunity, after 14 interviews and 2 days of strenuous work, I was offered a challenging job. I started working for an animation company that now belongs to DreamWorks, makers of a number of feature films, including *Shrek*. A short time later, I was promoted to Art Director, and two years later I became the company's General Artistic Director. We had 30 co-workers back then—now they have over 700. I was the only Latin American in the entire industry.

It was interesting to find out during a meeting that someone from Spain had been following my name since it was the only "Carlos" that was ever listed in the credits. The 90s came around, and many more people throughout Latin America became involved in the industry.

Learning through expansion

Demand in the 90s for videos and animation was exponential, so five of us were sent to open up branches throughout California. I spent the first year working in San Francisco and the second year working in Los Angeles. During that time, we made movies such as *Natural Born Killers*, directed by Oliver Stone and produced by Disney, followed by *Space Jam*, *Armageddon*, and the *Devil's Advocate*, among others. I also had the opportunity of working with Michael Bay, director of *Transformers* and *Batman and Robin*.

As many might know, innovation is key in this industry, however it's not something that comes easily.

Deciding to go into business for myself, and my first obstacles

The decision to undertake a new business venture was a combination of opportunity, the experience I had already acquired, and a genuine passion for the entertainment field and the creative industry. The U.S. was changing and so was I. I started thinking about my life's priorities, of how I wanted to impact the region's development, and so an idea was birthed out of this personal uneasiness. I dreamt of a Guatemala where young people could live in and experience a culture of innovation. Today, that dream is a reality—a young person can work in the movie field. At the time, however, this was unheard of.

I went back to Guatemala and founded Studio C as one of the pioneer movie studios of Latin America. I was based in Antigua, and no, it wasn't an easy venture to undertake. People bombarded me with statements such as "There's nothing like that here" or "You can't do that here." But then I thought, if at the age of 17 I was able to make it in the U.S. without a dime to my name, I knew that everything was possible. So I said to myself, "Where there's a will, there's a way!"

My first client was a social project. The Center for Mesoamerica Regional Research (CIRMA) had carried out a study on discrimination in Guatemala, and they wanted young people to learn more about the subject. We talked about how to convert the study into images and create a display.

In the next two years, we worked on a number of local projects, growing from 1 person to 30 co-workers, as well as relocating our exhibition center to Cuatro Grados Norte in Guatemala City.

International customers and culture clash

Our accelerated growth was due mainly to the wonderful contacts I had established throughout the previous two years. My first international client was Universal Studios. They awarded us part of the *The Chronicles of Riddick* project, starring Vin Diesel. Our second contract came from DreamWorks to work on *The Ring 2*, followed by the third *Fever Pitch* for Fox. These credentials quickly brought us new contracts in Universal films, such as special effects on *The Fast and the Furious*, many of them proudly made in Guatemala.

Understanding the film industry can be complicated. Contrarily, understanding special effects is a matter of one general rule: a film's overall budget generally allots 50% to special effects. Therefore, a full contract can average $50 million dollars split among the different companies that create the effects. Due to scale economics and pressures in cost optimization, production companies usually divide their budgets into different contracts, always keeping an eye on key indicators such as quality and deadlines. A delay in special effects can easily cost them millions. This is why it's an industry where teamwork is paramount; I must fully trust in what other people and teams are doing.

I must admit here that although I grew up with a Latin soul, I have an American brain and an American work ethic. It's hard to say no to things in Guatemala, and Guatemalans are constantly pestered with inner-communication issues. However, it's an issue we can't afford, since globalization demands a different type of work that's more connected and has better communication with others. That was perhaps the greatest culture shock barrier we had to overcome between Guatemalans and our American customers. "How can you want us to work over Easter break?" was a remark I once heard while working on an account. Americans were expecting delivery and we just couldn't be thinking on vacation, especially not with a business like ours that was starting to make a name for itself.

The search for talent

Finding qualified talent in a country like Guatemala for a virtually non-existent industry was a gargantuan task. We opted for hiring those with the best learning skills and developed our own methodologies.

The company that started off as an animations studio had to evolve into a number of other businesses as well. We had to develop new educational systems to train our talent. We had to strengthen our national culture. Thus, new company divisions gave way. In fact, we designed our own training manuals on how to teach and train the interns in the technology, paving the way for our work to start expanding into the public sector.

My personal learning difficulties allowed me to provide solid solutions for thousands of children. We collaborated in projects that would make learning mathematics a simple, interactive, and fun process. We carried out a project with *Boys Hope Girls Hope* from the U.S., using these interactive techniques to teach children from Zone 2 in our city.

Designing a prototype in the U.S. can run up to $1 million dollars, however the cost in Guatemala was over 40 times less.

With the growth of greater and larger endeavors, the search for talent became more difficult. I discovered that I had to work as a group, thinking in terms of Central America. I dreamt of a generation of young people that could produce high-quality material for videos, movies, and animations. This led us to opening Studio C branches in Mexico, Los Angeles, Costa Rica, Columbia, and of course, where it all first started—Guatemala.

I strongly believe that audiovisual industries as a developmental hub for a nation are becoming more and more important each passing day.

In Guatemala, I see an entire generation with the potential to work in technology and creativity. However, many young people that can help facilitate the transition are abroad, thus Guatemala must open it's doors to them since we can't do it alone. Connecting with other more developed countries is vital. Columbia and Mexico are clear examples of how the industry can develop. We need to speed up the learning process to further promote the transfer of knowledge.

The second hub I envision for the promotion of creative industries is risk capital. Advancement of this is vital for high-potential, new projects to come to light. I was greatly impressed by how in Mexico and Columbia, instead of paying taxes, one can invest in a movie. These incentives are being created for people to invest in the film industry in their countries and develop its growth. The National Learning Service of Columbia (SENA for short) is swiftly promoting education in the field. This is where the government is taking an active role. In fact, they are actually helping support Studio C in Columbia. In short, I have seen how people invest in the film industry, as the government invests in talent instruction.

In order to grow, Studio C is arduously working in co-productions with Mexico, Columbia, and the U.S. We have a film production crew working with Disney, which is helping us show the project's viability. Sure, the dream is big, but so is the need for accelerated learning and the exchange of better practices between countries.

A peek into the future

The interesting thing about the entertainment industry is that it grows the most during periods of crisis. Thanks to globalization, it's easier to convey subject matter visually, which is the reason why many industries are shifting toward audiovisual standards. Everything we teach our young people in Studio C doesn't just apply to film making, but also to the fields of teaching, fashion design, science, architecture, textiles, simulation, etc. It's one of the healthiest industries I know of. We started off as a Guatemalan company and became pioneers in the field, and we've combined young people with cutting-edge technology and made it a regional business.

I still remember those words, "He doesn't have the skills to study." Don't ever limit your dreams. We must learn to share our ideas, especially when we live in a world riddled with so much distrust. We must learn to come together and work as a region. Let's stop talking in terms of country and start thinking in terms of teams. Let's start envisioning our country projecting itself globally.

I see the world through a different lens, but that's just how I was born. Perhaps to many it was a problem, but for me it turned into the best tool I could have to successfully undertake new ventures.

And this is how Carlo Arguello talks about his undertaking, his passion combined with gifts, talents, and profitability. It has projected itself and transcended to incredible levels. What can we glean from his experience? What must we improve prior to undertaking a new business venture? What things can jeopardize the business we have in mind? Are you ready to take that leap into your new venture? Then the next stage is planning.

Just a thought before we begin

If I could summarize from my own life experiences the most important things I've learned throughout these last couple of years, it's that your motive for wanting to undertake a new enterprise will either make or break the initial stages in the voyage. Businesses that transcend are birthed out of a powerful cause, clearly articulating the problem they wish to solve. Businesses that fail are those quickly motivated by myths such as, "I can make more money with my own business," "That way I can be my own boss" or "That way I can manage my time, my way." We now know that these are half-truths at best since the fact is that any undertaking is going to require great effort, conviction, and passion.

Asking ourselves to honestly describe what our dream is forces us to reflect on our purpose, our passion, and our talents. Rarely if ever will a person honestly say that their sole drive is to make money or escape from an imperious and domineering boss. Yet in order to be successful, we must really put our feet on the ground and embrace what we're about to face by launching our venture. So let's get to work!

From Dream to Reality: The Business Plan

Those that don't risk anything can save themselves trouble and hurt.
But they will never learn, grow, feel, change and love.
– Eileen Caddy

Strategizing is more an art than it is a science. Millions of books on strategy are penned every year, yet the principles remain the same. I've taken the liberty of summarizing the theory of strategy in a model I've named "Julio Zelaya's Model on Strategy: Scan, Select and Execute." My goal is that you apply it by answering a few questions and taking solid action steps. At the end of this section, you'll find an outline of a business plan that you can apply for your idea.

Scan

The purpose of the scanning stage is to identify opportunities all around you, in other words—items that can help your business. It also serves to identify threats all around you, all those things that could hurt or jeopardize your business. A final purpose is to high-light your strengths and weaknesses as a businessperson and those of your business idea. For that, you will use a SWOT evaluation (described below). Many of the elements in this analysis are mentioned throughout the book, but this is where we put it all together. Answer the following questions in your notebook and list the options you have for each one.

- What is your business model? Another way of viewing this is that if you needed to explain it to someone who knew absolutely nothing about your business, how would you explain it?

- Do you have the right people to start your business? Do you have the minimum talent required to begin operations?
- Do you have access to resources? I'm not speaking about having all the work capital or money at once, but to at least have access to it through loans, relatives, savings, credit, or other means.
- Do you have at least ten clients available that are interested in your product or service?
- What are the key components for your start up? In a food enterprise, you might need a health license, and in technology it might be a business license or patent.
- Do you have these items at your disposal? If not, when will you have them?
- Do you have access to sound legal advice?
- Do you have access to reliable tax and accounting advice?

Write down what at least ten potential clients have said about your business idea. If you haven't gone out into the real world to validate your idea, then now is the time to do so. Copy this table in your notebook and complete the exercise.

Name of potential customer #1:
Positive things he said:
Negative things he said:
Notes about our conversation:

Name of potential customer #2:
Positive things he said:
Negative things he said:
Notes about our conversation:

Name of potential customer #3:
Positive things he said:
Negative things he said:
Notes about our conversation:

SWOT analysis

The SWOT analysis is a research methodology used to determine the internal and external situations of a company to better assess their strengths, weaknesses, opportunities, and threats. A company's internal situation is made up of two controllable factors: strengths and weaknesses, whereas the external situation is composed of two non-controllable factors: opportunities and threats.

Examples of Strengths:

- I possess a degree in business administration
- I have enough saved up allowing me to go without an income for three years

Examples of Weaknesses:

- I have a poor credit rating for a loan
- I can't speak English well, and I wish to do business in the U.S.

Examples of Opportunities:

- A new law promoting new businesses is about to be enacted
- Investment in the area you wish to launch your startup is increasing at a rate of 50% per year

Examples of Weaknesses

- There is a risk of a prolonged recession
- Oil prices are going up

With all the information you've compiled so far, fill out a SWOT analysis for your business and a separate one for you as an entrepreneur. Please do not take this exercise lightly. Remember what Sun Tzu wrote, "Whatever you sweat in the training field, you won't bleed in the battle field." This exercise can help to greatly determine your success or failure in a business.

Selection

A dream fulfilled rejoices the soul.
– Proverbs 13:19

Once you reach the selection stage, you must then define your strategy. What will you do? What won't you do? These are the two most important questions when devising a business strategy. It's easy to define what you *will* do in your business, yet hardly ever do you sit down to specify what you *won't* do. Remember, once your business becomes successful, your opportunities will expand. People will approach you to offer alliances, partnerships, or new products or services. Your strategy will set the stage to know when to say yes and when to say no.

A strategy is a set of actions carried out for a specific end. It comes from the Greek word ΣΤΡΑΤΗΓΙΚΗΣ (stratos), which in turn has its roots in army and agent, conductor and guide. In short, it answers the question, "How will we do it?" Let's look at a case study on strategy and its importance when choosing alternatives.

Tony Fadell, an entrepreneur, brought a potential idea to Apple: a digital audio player. Following his hiring as an independent consultant and nine-month assignment to perfect the idea, on October 23rd, 2001, Apple launched the revolutionary iPod into the market.

By November 2008, over 175 million units had been sold worldwide. In 2005 and 2006, iPod sales represented 58% of Apple's total revenue growth. By 2008, it represented an overall average of 21% sales growth. Apple's iPod sales are a multi-billion-dollar business. According to Business Week, iPod has created an accessories industry valued at over 1 billion dollars in the U.S. alone. Multiple items, such as cases, headphones, FM modulators, clothing accessories, car interfaces, sound systems, speakers, and others are manufactured year-round. It's estimated that the market for accessories grows at a much faster pace than that of iPod sales. If you were Steve Jobs, Apple's CEO, wouldn't you have been tempted to design iPod accessories? This is a clear example of determining and setting your strategy. Steve Jobs' responsibility was to say no in spite of the tantalizing temptation to enter into this highly profitable market. Mr. Jobs simply said, "That's not the business we're in" and continued to focus on Apple's core objective, now known to all: "Creating tools for creative minds."

How do you manage your business? Do you say yes to every opportunity that comes your way, or do you know how to choose in accordance to your predefined strategy? The role a strategy plays is to choose between alternatives. If you analyze Apple's model, you'll find that they have clearly defined who their customer is, the need they meet, the prices they'll charge, and even more importantly, how they'll achieve it. They're always asking, "What is our business?" This in turn allows them to filter through the viable and attractive alternatives that will keep them focused.

In order to better define your strategy, answer the following questions:

- What specific need do I meet?
- Who is the customer?
- What price do I offer?
- How will I produce it?
- What business am I in?

Before answering these questions for your business undertaking, let's do the following exercise.

In 1998, Puma was practically a non-existent business on the verge of going broke. Germany alone had a few fans that still purchased their shoes. Nike and Adidas were the undisputed leaders worldwide. Puma wasn't fashion footwear, nor was it even on the radar.

That same year, one of the most dramatic restructurings a business could undergo took place. Armed with a deep market knowledge, team Puma noticed that more and more young people were less interested in high-performance shoes and more interested in them as a fashion statement. So Jochen Zeits, Puma CEO, asked himself a wide array of questions. We'll use the following model to analyze it.

What is the need?
- High performance shoes
- Feel and look good in a stylish shoe

Who's the customer?
- Athletes
- Young people wanting to look trendy and in-style

What is the relative price?
- Similar to the competition.
- Higher than the competition

How will we do it?
- Research in sports technology
- Contracting fashion designers Philippe Starck and Jil Sander
- Get the shoe known through celebrities

What business am I in?
- Sports shoes
- Fashion

Now let's apply the four dimensional assessment proposed by Chan Kim and Mauborgne in the book *Blue Ocean Strategy*. The result: Puma reinvented the tennis shoe in Europe and in the rest of the world. Their strategy turned the company around from one on the verge of bankruptcy to one generating billions of dollars annually. Businesses such as Gucci, Dolce & Gabanna, DKNY, and Prada followed this trend within a complete industry created by Puma: the sports fashion shoe.

> *Questions are more important than answers.*
> *– Francisco "Pancho" García (Founder of Pancho & Company)*

These were some of the things Puma analyzed:

What must we **ELIMINATE?**	What must we **INCREASE?**
Technological features of the shoe itself.	Brand recognition
	Innovation capacity
Boring packaging	Investment in selective and targeted ad campaigns
What must we **REDUCE?**	What must we **CREATE?**
	Stylish designs
Number of shoe models	
	Tennis shoe inclusion in fashion shows
Investment in massive advertising campaigns	
	Eye-catching packaging

Puma reinvented its business by asking nine key questions:

Question	Definition
What need do I meet?	What problem do I solve for my customer?
	How can I add value to my customer?
What customers do I wish to serve?	Who is my client?
	How will they purchase my product or service?
	Where will they purchase my product or service?
	How many customers are we talking about?
What relative price will I charge?	How much is a customer willing to pay for my product or service?
	Specifically how much would they be willing to pay for the need or problem I solve?
	How will they pay for it?
How will I do it?	What will my strategy be?
	How will I be different from others?
	How can I make the customer aware of the problem I'm solving?

What business am I in?	What am I really selling?
	Ask yourself this in your customer's shoes, not from your stance. For example, if you were selling electric drills, then you're basically in the "hole" business.
What must we eliminate in the business?	What must you completely eliminate from your service proposal to meet your strategy?
	What must you eliminate that the customer doesn't value?
What must we increase in the business?	According to what the customer values, what must we increase and what processes must we eliminate?
What must we cut down in the business?	What must we reduce or minimize that doesn't add much customer value?
What must we create in the business?	What doesn't exist yet that would add value to the customer?
	What else is needed in the business?

Which of the following strategies is closest to your business?

Question	Operational Efficiency	Strategic Efficiency
Definition	Faster than the competition	Exceptional customer value
	Cheaper than the competition	Unique perceived value, different from competitors
Implementation	Easier: Purchased with competitors Less customer knowledge.	More complicated: Nothing to compare with Greater customer insight.
Profitability	Slightly higher than the competition's.	Greater because business sets the margin according to the problem they solve. Greater risk.

I know that we've asked ourselves certain things to help define our business, starting off with our dreams. However, I urge you to answer the following questions with a strategic mindset, taking into account that you have now clearly identified the business you want to open. These answers are foundational to your business plan, just as they were to Puma's.

- What need do I meet?
- What customer do I wish to serve?
- What relative price will I charge?
- How will I do it?
- What business am I really in?
- What must we eliminate in the business?
- What must we increase in the business?
- What must we reduce in the business?
- What must we create in the business?

Execution

A solid deed is worth more than a world of promises.
– Jacob Howell

The purpose of a business plan is to tell a story, to tell your business story. The plan must set forth a business opportunity worthy of exploring and executing. It must detail how to make the most of it and how to make it profitable. Moreover, designing a business plan will help you minimize certain temptations when executing it and launching your startup.

Temptation #1: Loving the business. A business plan helps you identify risks and opportunities to prepare for them.

Temptation #2: Over-optimism. Entrepreneurs tend to believe they'll do better than they possibly will. A business plan that's been shared and measured by others will help avoid blind spots.

Temptation #3: Building a business for the entrepreneur alone. Many times we end up solving problems that only we have. A business plan will help confirm if there are more customers facing the same issue.

Temptation #4: If you build it they'll come. It's a common temptation to believe that you'll get sales just for the sake of it. This is why it's important to validate potential customers. Do I really have a shot at selling my product?

Temptation #5: Poor initial products and services. Every business needs to have a balance between product volume (items more readily sold in important monthly amounts) and product margin (they sell more slowly, but still contribute strongly to the company's bottom line). At times, there's a tendency to over-depend on one type of product or service.

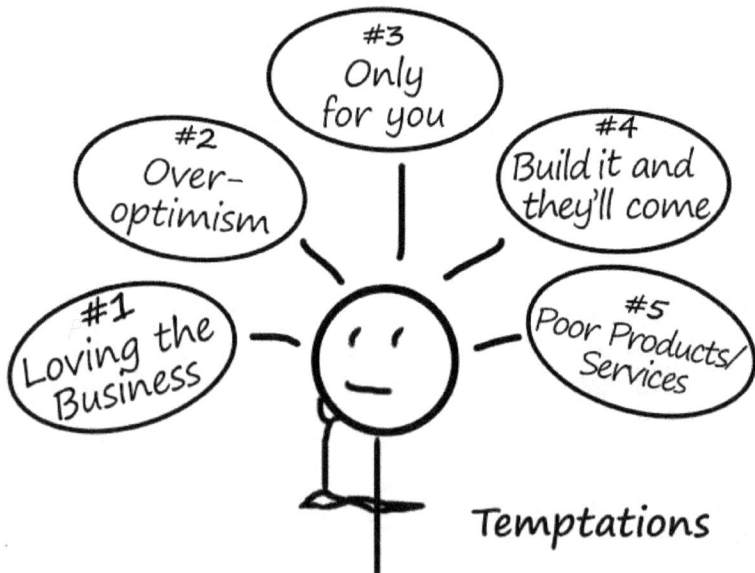

On one occasion, a college friend told me how he had devised a complex 80-page business plan, describing a company that would distribute medicine through online orders. The plan answered every single question a potential investor might ask, including detailed sales projections and market studies. An opportunity came up with a well-known investor who had agreed to meet him at the airport in his private jet. My friend had a presentation ready on his laptop and had made three copies of the business plan.

He had estimated an hour to explain the entire undertaking, risks, and earning potential. Once aboard, the investor cut right to the chase and said, "Welcome. As of this moment you have exactly three minutes to tell me your business idea. My colleague here (pointing to the person next to him) will keep time." My friend babbled and fumbled through his thoughts quickly, but was barely able to present the idea. Exactly 180 seconds later, the time was up and he said, "I wanted to teach you a lesson today. If your business plan is clear and concise, three minutes is all you need to make a convincing presentation. Don't ever forget it."

My friend said, "He taught me that you never know when you're going to meet a potential partner. If you were to bump into him in an elevator, you would have a maximum of three minutes to share your idea."

My colleague did get a second opportunity with the investor who ended up purchasing 60% of the business, and today they're involved in a number of undertakings together. What would happen if all you had were three minutes to present your idea?

Businessplan outline - The eight questions

I've gone over more business plans than I can imagine. I've interviewed investors in all parts of the world. They usually make their decisions based on the executive summaries of long contracts, usually designed by entrepreneurs. I once sold my business just sketching the basic parts of it on a sheet of paper. In fact, I've even designed entire business ventures on a sheet of paper. The model I'm about to show you is one I designed and have used on countless projects. They are eight basic questions that sum up your business model. Please answer them in your notebook.

Now imagine that you were to make a brief business plan for Apple's iWatch. The examples listed in the right column show the importance of researching and using factual data.

What problem do I solve?	Every undertaking is designed to solve a problem, fill a need, take on a challenge. Define the problem in one sentence.	Link fashion with connectivity
How large is the problem?	What size is the market? How many people are facing the same dilemma you envision?	According to Strategy Analytics, it's estimated that the market for fashion devices was 1 million units for 2014 and could reach up to 5 million units for 2015.
How do I solve the problem?	Define a specific, solid solution to meet the need mentioned above. State it in one sentence.	A fashion watch that can connect to your iPhone with similar functions to that of a computer.
How do I better solve this problem than the competition or substitutes?	Every undertaking has direct competition and substitutes. I've yet to find a case where this isn't true. What competition or substitute do you offer and how is it better than the rest?	Unique interface (Digital Crown) Proprietary operating system (iWatch OS) Interactive proprietary technology (Force Touch, haptics) More sensors than the competition.
How do I make money with it?	What are your sources of income? Every for profit or not-for-profit venture requires and manages resources. Where will the money come from?	Revenue from the watch per se (three versions -Watch, Sport, Edition) Estimated 60% gross margin over sales price. iWatch price range between $349 and $17,000. Average iWatch price estimated at $499 for first trimester sales. Revenue from 3rd. party applications (earnings model allotment is 70% for developer and 30% for Apple.) 5,000 new apps expected for first trimester of launch.

		There are over 600 million iPhones (captive market awaiting iWatch)Intellectual property ready to be marketed in various watch components.
Why I? (US)	What qualifies you and your team to solve this problem? Credibility is important for any undertaking.	Current production capacity at over 5 million units annually.
Why now?	Why should you launch this venture right now? Analyze the time variable and how the opportunity links up with the immediate timing.	Growth estimate for the smart watch market in 2015 is estimated at 457% per year.
What do I want?	This question is commonly overlooked. It's the hard core request itself. What am I expecting? Startup capital? A client? An associate? Be specific in your requests	Authorization for product launch, from prototype to large scale sales.

Elevator version

Great things aren't achieved on the stage of impulse, but as the sum of small little steps joined together.
– Vincent van Gogh

If you only had 180 seconds to present the answers to all 8 questions, what would you say? Read your answers aloud.

From business plan to an emporium: Kenneth Cole Productions

When Kenneth Cole wanted to start his business, he lacked sufficient financing. He did, however, know that it was easier to get credit in Europe than it was in U.S. banks. He located those factories in Europe and designed a shoe collection with the intent of returning to the U.S. to sell them. The pressure of having to pay his creditors was high, so he had to sell his vast production as soon as possible.

The company now known as Kenneth Cole Productions Inc. was originally birthed in 1982 as Kenneth Cole Incorporated, however the name change was a result of an ingenious marketing strategy. The firm's creator had originally planned on displaying his shoe line at Market Week, the most prestigious shoe event in the city at New York's Hilton Hotel, but he was unable to afford the purchase for a showroom. He also knew that it was going to be difficult to get known as a new designer among a thousand other companies on display. So he came up with the following idea: park a semi-trailer display in front of the Hilton in order to draw the attention of those present for Market Week.

Putting his plan into play required changing the name of his company in the next two hours, because permits were only issued to production companies. So on December 2nd, 1982, with permit in hand, he parked his trailer in front of the Hilton Hotel, equipped with the very best shoe store, all the while filming the full-length feature film *The Birth of a Shoe Company*. To complete the masquerade, he rented an entire film crew complete with director, lighting, cameras, models, and even two New York police officers securing the area. Thus he was able to sell 40,000 pairs of shoes in just 2 ½ days—his entire production line.

What have we done up until now? By summarizing the stages we've covered up to this moment, we have:

- Pinpointed what we love doing and have a passion for
- Identified our key talents
- Combined these items with our purpose
- Defined a few variables that will help us live off this purpose
- Analyzed how to turn this purpose into a startup
- Designed a business plan for our undertaking

The task has been an intense one, but also a lonely one. So should I launch my venture? Now is when the plan comes to life, and we go from I, Inc. to Us, Inc.

2

Us, Inc.

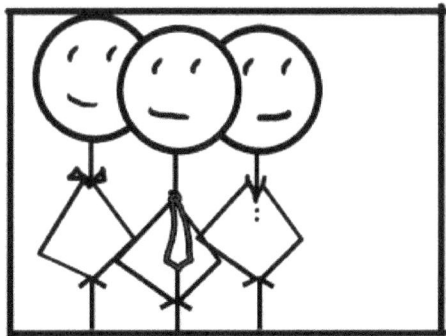

We all are entrepreneurs, but few of us have the chance to practice it.
– Muhammad Yunus

Starting is half of everything.
– Ptagoras de Samos

A few years ago, I had the opportunity of interviewing Walter de la Cruz, founder of Cafe Barista in Guatemala. His success story is fascinating and has served to inspire many, wanting to transition from an **I, Inc.** to **Us, Inc.** Read and you'll see why.

From I, Inc. to Us, Inc.: Walter de la Cruz's Story

I searched for my coffee shop's first location, fully aware that this would be the first main obstacle to overcome. In every interview I had with managers of shopping centers and malls, they all asked me the same thing, "Where can we see one in operation?" Lacking neither a first locale nor a history of operating businesses in that market made it difficult, if not impossible, to secure a venue.

I was finally able to rent part of a house located at 16 Calle y 4a. Avenida Zone 14. I remember going there with our interior designer and thinking, *There's not a soul in sight, not even a car.* It was a completely residential area with hardly any traffic at all. However, when I walked through the venue, I suddenly felt a good vibe. I really can't say what made that location our first coffee shop, but I just felt it was right. I knew deep down that it would be a success. And it was vital to open this first shop in order to start negotiating other possible locations.

We signed the lease and got ready to start operations on November 12th, 2004. But we were still missing furniture. I got some estimates, none lower than $5,000 and others way over my budget. My brother-in-law, who was living in Virginia, suggested I visit an IKEA furniture store in the States. I traveled the next day and arrived in Virginia on Saturday night. Come 10:00 a.m. Sunday morning, we were at the local IKEA shop with a 22-foot truck.

Walking through the store and seeing its prices allowed me to furnish not just one but three coffee shops. About 12 hours later we were done shopping, and I'll never forget the cashier's expression. "I've never sold so much to one customer," she said. The store manager, a Dutch lady, upon seeing how much we had purchased, had everyone in her store help carry the items out to the sidewalk. By 3:00 a.m., my brother-in-law and I had finished loading the truck. We arrived at the storage unit at 5:00 a.m. and by 7:00 a.m. we were back home. My brother-in-law took a nap, and I took a shower for my flight back to Guatemala.

I still remember that day like it was just yesterday. No doubt I owe him a huge favor because that was one tough weekend. Today, all our furniture is manufactured here in Guatemala of the utmost quality by a local manufacturer and at a comfortable price.

Shortly before opening, Cafe Barista hired its first staff member. The job was becoming virtually impossible for me alone. My wife recommended a lady, Ms. Silvia Santizo, who had recently resigned from Cementos Progreso's museum department and was in search of new employment. We met, I explained our business model, and she loved the idea. I told her, "I just have two conditions for this opening: someone willing to work hard and to not be a crybaby."

"Well, I work hard, and I don't cry," came the reply.

"You're hired!" And just like that, without any formal protocol, our first HR manager came into the team.

Finding qualified talent was indeed a challenge, just as with large corporations. Yet, there was a certain glow about working in a café, despite the sacrifices it entailed. I've always sought to do things openly, honestly, and transparently. We started drawing good personnel, despite our wages being low back then. We decided to share in the success by implementing a compensation model made up of 2% overall sales distributed among our managers, assistant managers, and personnel. This was part of our success right from the start.

First day of operations

The day finally arrived, and on Friday, November 12, 2004, Cafe Barista opened for business. We were only open for about four hours because electrical glitches caused us to close shop earlier than expected. That day we sold an espresso to one customer and various other coffee beverages to my closest "clients:" my mom, wife, mother-in-law, and dad. Total sales for the day were approximately Q112[1]. However, thanks to that one espresso we sold, come Monday morning we had that same customer back in our coffee shop with three other friends saying, "This is the place where I've had the best coffee in all Guatemala."

On Saturday, November 13th, I had scheduled an electrician for 7:00 a.m. to make the necessary repairs. It was just me in the shop until around 8:00 a.m. when I heard a knock on the window. I opened the door, and this lady says, "Are you open?"

"I'm sorry, but we won't be open until Monday because of electrical problems."

"Oh no, this can't be. I saw your new coffee shop yesterday and told all my friends to meet us here. I can't say no, now." No sooner had she finished saying that when a few more vehicles arrived with six ladies and ten children in tow.

---

[1] Exchange rate was Q7.79 for $1.00

"If you make yourself at home and you're a little patient, I can get you that coffee, but remember—it's only me here today," I explained.

"But were going to get a little hungry," she hinted with a smile. That day, with just those customers alone, I made sales of over Q600 in sandwiches, coffee, eggs, and beverages. That amusing group of ladies left later that afternoon, and I closed up shop. I was totally exhausted, having worked every single store position there was: waiter, cashier, cook, manager, and of course, barista.

To this day, I'm pleased with having served them that Saturday morning. Consequently, they're still some of my best customers, and I greatly appreciate them.

The rest of the days, right up to November 17, we opened on an irregular basis. Sales in 2004 were low, but starting January they started picking up. Almost overnight, we had turned in to the place to be and that was just beginning.

Hearing Walter taught me a lot about a business's beginnings and confirmed my conviction that passion is one of the most deciding factors for success. Today, Cafe Barista is part of Multi Inversiones Corporation, one of Latin America's largest holding companies in the following industries: flour, cookies, pastas, restaurant franchises such as Pollo Campero, energy, and construction. Walter's still an executive board member of Barista and has also founded other businesses as well, such as the Carmen and Brickhouse restaurants.

This second section of Us, Inc. is dedicated to a startup's launch, when we stop being a company of one and become a group of people working together toward a common goal. This is the hiring stage, which can be done either onsite or via digital tools. The time has come to launch your new venture. Perhaps you've already resigned from your day job or you're investing significant resources into your undertaking. If you are an entrepreneur within a business, this is when the business enters the prototype stage, ready to be launched.

While it's true that everything is birthed from a dream, the time also comes when that dream starts to enter the implementation phase and become reality. This is the stage when we need to press forward in our focus and see our business beyond ourselves. We go from the I, Inc. phase into the Us, Inc. It's also the stage where an organizational structure is required as well as involvement of more visionaries that share in our enthusiasm of making this entrepreneurial idea a full-fledged reality.

Consider the following examples of entrepreneurs in this stage:

- Two partners started a food processing plant but they underestimated the time it would take to process a sanitary license. One-hundred percent of their clientele required this to do business with them.
- An entrepreneur seeking to save on legal expenses left out the "right of first refusal" clause in the corporation charter, only to later find out the hard way when part of his business was sold away.
- A business imported games from China only to later find out, once already in the market, that no one understood how they worked. None were sold, despite much market research assuring them that it was a definite sell.
- A business venture that was so successful in the first six months, it ran out of a projected three-year supply of inventory.
- A business that was so successful that it went bankrupt after two years for lacking enough working capital to keep up with the accelerated growth.
- A business venture where the founder hired an accountant without checking his references, only to find out a year later that he had neither graduated from college nor did he know anything about the field, costing him over $60,000 in fines for improper tax filings. (I know this firsthand—it was me.)

When we first start a business, there's a tendency to make affirmations such as the following:

- "This won't happen to me."
- "My business is different, unlike others that have gone under."
- "My partner and I are friends; what can go wrong."
- "They'll start buying once we open."
- "There's no problem with me not having a set salary; I'll just take money out whenever I need some."
- "I'll just handle the books for now. Once we grow, we'll do it seriously."
- "There are many successful family-owned businesses; why bore them with the rules of the game."
- "There's no need to have enough for the first six months; I'm sure sales will pick up from the moment we open."

Us, Inc. is the stage where we invite others on the journey of our business: family, friends, fellow-workers, clients, and creditors. It's the stage that validates in real life what up until now had just been an idea we've been believing in. We must make sure to take every variable and outlook into account in this stage. Remember, now there are others counting on this venture also, not just you. This is why in this section we'll look at different variables and tools to develop your undertaking.

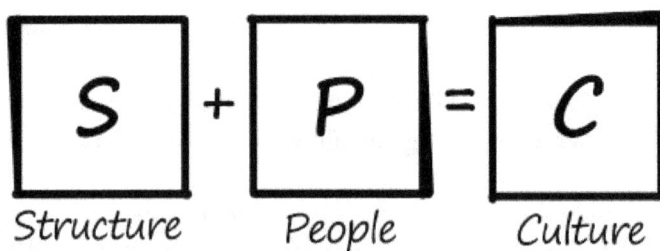

$$\boxed{S} + \boxed{P} = \boxed{C}$$

Structure   People   Culture

Us, Inc.'s Three Variables

I was recently going over Martin Scorsese's well-known movie *Hugo*. Hugo Cabret—its main character—envisioned the world as one large machine, and that each one of us had a specific and unique purpose within it. He would get immensely sad whenever a machine would break down because it could no longer fulfill its purpose. He compared it to how many times the same thing can happen to people. They can lose their purpose or bearing on what they were made for.

Structure

Just like a machine has its own specific structural design and operation, so does every undertaking. Consequently, an undertaking must be set up and organized according to its purpose. No wonder the most successful circus in the world—Cirque Du Soleil—is structured by people dedicated to creativity; or that Apple has their design department report directly to the CEO. A business's structure must answer the question as to how to the startup is to reach its goals.

People - The right people first, then everything else

Jim Collins was the first person to popularize the phrase, "First who, then what." He carried out a study in different types of enterprises: public and private, big and small. The principle applies to every type of undertaking, and many start-ups have got to solve both the who and the what at the same time.

When we speak about people, we're referring to the necessary talent pivotal to an organization. These are the people that will build the enterprise in addition to those that start it together with the founder. Hiring the right people at the beginning of any endeavor is quite complicated but crucial for success. I know what you're thinking, "How can I ever afford the right people if I can barely cover my own basic expenses?" Don't worry, we'll be talking about this subject throughout the rest of the book. Microsoft wouldn't be Microsoft if Bill Gates did not have Paul Allen. Apple would have never reached its potential if Steve Jobs hadn't had Steve Wozniak. Start-ups and undertakings aren't individual sports; they need a team.

It's common for every new venture to compare itself to well-established corporations and think, *When will I ever reach that level?* We are aware that we need the whole package: clients, staff, money, systems, marketing, supplies, and work capital as well as a number of other things that you didn't even imagine when you first designed your business plan.

Nevertheless, don't ever forget the ever-important human factor. Your undertaking's success will always depend on the passion that you and your team reflect. Launching isn't the same as conceptualizing because nothing is ever static, but always remember that first comes the dreamer, then the dream. Regardless of how small you might think your undertaking is at the beginning, if you have the right associates and fellow-workers, your growth is pretty much guaranteed.

No business ever started with the model they ended up with. Do you think that Google learned how to make money just a few years into their venture? The original idea they had was around selling search engines, which even Yahoo turned down. The great Steve Jobs had to rethink his model and the right products for Apple over and over again. But he was able to make it, thanks to the right people with whom to share the risks, the plans, the prototypes, the workload, and the responsibilities.

Culture - How we do things

Have you ever noticed how there are some organizations with a very solid culture? It almost seems as if the moment you walk through their door you've entered into another country. By culture, I mean that every company has its own:

- Communication code (words, even gestures commonly used)

- Dress code
- Symbolism
- Implicit and explicit values
- Heroes and villains (those they reward and those they punish)
- Systems of reward and admonition
- Basic core beliefs

Culture tends to be the intangible variable that determines whether or not you achieve your strategy. How does Zappos have such great service? How does Apple innovate so much? What causes a country to develop and others not to, even when they share the same border? Culture is the ever-defining variable that explains this.

Now then, let's see each one of the elements with their proper tools.

Structure

> *When you start things off right, you're half way there.*
> *– Fernando de Rojas*

When I was about 12 years old, I saw my dad very worried about something. I went with him to the safety deposit box at the bank to pick up some deeds. With an expression of sheer affliction, we then proceeded to another bank where he had a pending credit card debt and handed over the deeds to the house. "Dad, you owe an entire house!" I cried out. I remember admonishing him. How could he have fallen into debt so irresponsibly?

Time went by and when I was 26 years old, I had made poor decisions on whom to partner with and lost virtually all of my assets. Unemployed, I was forced to face the one situation I most feared in life: consolidate my debts and pay them off. I used to rip up my bank statements in annoyance. "Yes, I know I owe you; why even bother opening them?" I'd get defensive every time someone spoke about money management.

After I had opened up every envelope and tallied up every debt, I owed almost $100,000 to credit cards. I remember telling my wife, "I owe an entire house!" Right there and then, I recalled the words I so carelessly expressed to my dad when I was a child. What I promised would never happen to me was taking place before my very eyes. I was angry with myself, I recused myself, but I also started recognizing that it had been the fruit of my own decisions, my own arrogance, and my lack of discipline.

I made a visible list of my debts. I ordered them from the smallest to the largest and placed them in areas where I'd be forced to look at them every day: in my office, at the bottom of computer screen, in the bathroom. I even mentioned them sometimes in the classes I taught in college. Some people asked me, "How can you put yourself out there like that?" But I promise you, it was one of the decisions that has helped me most in life. Publicly acknowledging my situation made me all the more committed to rectifying it.

Having chosen to face the situation, I remember locking myself in my room and confessing to God in prayer, "I feel powerless to get out of this; please help me." It was a humbling moment of having to recognize that I couldn't do it alone, but at the same time, I was willing to work hard to resolve it.

I went to the banks that I owed, and bringing to mind a phrase my dad said many times when I was growing up, "Your name is the greatest asset you have son, take care of it," I spoke with those in charge and laid bare my situation, assuring them that I would indeed pay it all off. I told them that one day I would be an important customer in their bank, that I would rise back up again, and that all I was asking was for them not to stain my credit. I would periodically stop by, updating them on my progress and making payments every chance I got.

Today, a number of years later, I can proudly say that my debt is paid off. I have a great credit rating and no stain to my name. Although it wasn't easy, it was a process where I definitely saw the hand of God move on my behalf.

Now why do I share this with you? I always knew that in time my credit and good name would be a valuable asset. My short-term decisions would be crucial in the long run.

That's the essence of this section. Once you make up your mind to start a business and you design your company's structure, you need to think in the long-term because you never know if the business you're founding might become the next multi-national corporation employing thousands of people. As a former IBM executive used to say, "Make decisions today as if you already had a large business."

Structuring your business requires the best consulting you can get because many times a lack of experience can hinder your ability to see the implications of your decision-making process. What fiscal strategy should you pursue? What clauses should you include in your incorporation papers? What type of partner are you looking for? How should you set up the shares? Who should be your legal representative? How will you assemble your board? How should you start the sales process? How should you start operations? How much money will you need now and in the future?

Take the necessary time to answer these questions. If you're going to have partners, then focus on these questions as a group and write down your answers. Remember the words of Sun Tzu, "What you sweat in the training field, you won't bleed in the battle field."

The three stages of any startup

David Thompson wrote a book, *Blueprint to a Million*, where he summarized Dr. David Birch's research on companies. He found that there are three key moments that all businesses go through, and the decisions made in them greatly define the type of business it will become. Look at the following model.

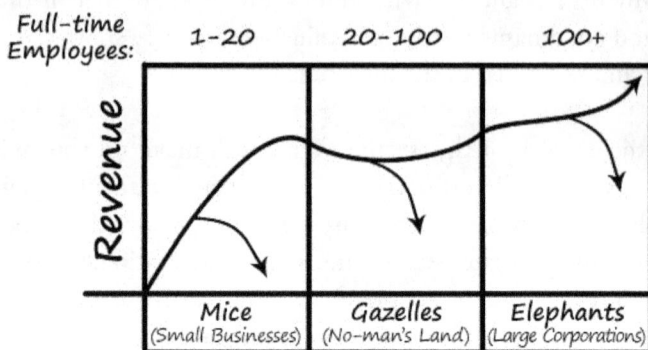

Full-time Employees:	1-20	20-100	100+

Mice (Small Businesses) | Gazelles (No-man's Land) | Elephants (Large Corporations)

You'll notice three crucial moments here:

Moment	Priorities
Mouse / Small Business Startup (1–20 full time employees) (0–$1 million in sales) High rate of failure	Survive. Find recurring sales and healthy markups.
Gazelles Business growth (20–100 full time employees) ($1–10 million in sales) They're neither small nor large. That's why they're called "No-mans Land." Notwithstanding they grow at an accelerated rate, over 20% annually for the next 4 years.	Consolidate the management team. Seek scalability and replication. Discover new sources of financing to grow.
Elephant/Large Corporation Business consolidation (100+ full time employees) ($10 million or more in sales)	Consolidate the business culture. Develop innovative mechanisms. Manage corporate government and complex financial strategies.

Notice how complex it is to research businesses; the scales are all over the board. You can use this to pinpoint your business through any of two criteria: by number of full-time employees or by annual billing in U.S. dollars. I know what you're thinking now: it depends on the country, the industry, and the product. As with every model, it's an approximation for the purpose of analysis.

Each phase has its own priorities, as you can see from the table. As an entrepreneur, you must focus on those critical moments to learn to recognize them.

Navigating through these stages requires analysis of four critical factors: market, management, model, and money. Doug Tatum delves into these stages in his book *No Man's Land*. Look at each one more closely and copy this table in your notebook.

Component	How does this apply to my startup?	How do I apply it to my undertaking?
Market	What is my target market? Who is my real customer?	
Management	Do I have the qualified personnel to manage growth and the future of my venture?	
Model	Is my business idea scalable and replicable? Can I implement it in other countries and regions profitably and in a consistent manner of time?	
Money	Do I have a way of getting more money to grow my business?	

When you first start a business, all you want is that first sale. But believe me when I tell you that it's just as important to open up the business itself and not have even your parents or friends buy from you (not make a single sale), then to sell to everything that moves (high sales). Growth and management are crucial to any undertaking, and you must prepare for it.

In my work with other investors, the question concerning their business model is one that continually comes up. It's common to find businesses solely relying on the entrepreneur and never searching for strategies to make the business grow, in spite of the founder. Allow me to make this analogy: If a barber goes into business based on his fame as a stylist, the size of his business will be limited to his time availability with customers. However, if his plan is to open up franchises training dozens of barbers in his particular techniques, then the size of the business will be directly proportionate to the number of franchises he opens.

Consider and answer the following questions in your notebook.

Market	Management	Model	Money
Describe as detailed as possible who your target customers are, what needs you solve for them, and how much they are willing to pay to meet that need.	What are your strengths as a manager? Are you a natural salesman or a natural administrator? Who should you hire first to better complement you? How do you plan to draw these people?	If you were to sell to one million customers, how would you do it? How can you run your business in ten countries at the same time? How can you keep your business from having to depend on you?	If you had to get $100,000, how would you do it? How would you get $1 million, $10 million? Write down the maximum amount of money you could get right now, taking into account all of the possible options listed above.

Now with these answers, it's time draw an outline of how to set up your business.

How to design a structure

In recent years, I've seen an increasing trend in business restructuring. In the past, business structures used to be function-based such as: financial, operations, manufacturing, sales, and others. With the passing of time, however, those structures turned more into parent companies with double reporting. Currently, business structures are more horizontal, multinodal, with multiple reporting. Organizations have adapted to a multi-tasking world that demands shorter reply times.

How should you set up your business structure? It all depends on your strategy. What do you wish to achieve in the long term? Your organization should be set up accordingly.

Your structure throughout time

In order to properly plan a business's success, the questions you're frequently going to ask are, "How many years should I give the company to see if it's profitable?" and "What should I focus on in my company as time goes on?" To answer these questions, we'll use work done by Nichole Torres from *Entrepreneur Magazine* as a basis.

Six months after opening. The first six months of a business tend to be unpredictable because it's the first time the alleged business plans are put to the test. After the first six months, you should begin keeping a record of your processes, as well as defining who your target customers are, what the business does and doesn't do, and how to beat the competition. In other words, the operational part of the business should be flowing smoothly.

Also, by this time you'll have validated if your business model works. It's common in this initial phase to make changes to your original strategy or refine assumptions. *How do I know if I've reached this point?* Your business starts to have recurrent purchases, and your products or services become more consistent, offering the same quality in the majority of cases. So what should I focus on? The term is consolidation. Break down and analyze what works and what doesn't. Focus on what does work. Assess if what doesn't work can be corrected or should be eliminated altogether from the business. Write your conclusions down in your notebook.

12–18 months after opening. By this time, the majority of businesses that survive will have reached a stage of profitability. At the very least, it should be breaking even. By now, you should be in control of your business's operation and be able to identify the key areas that will make your business more lucrative. *How do I know if I've reached this point?* You'll be able to evaluate your profit and loss statement and know if your company is in the black. Another way of seeing it is if what you bill a customer is less than the cost of getting that customer in the first place. *What should I focus on?* Refining controls. Open an emergency fund for your business. Analyze where to cut needless costs and how to consolidate and improve earnings. Write down your conclusions about your startup in your notebook.

3–5 years after opening. By this time, you should be more effective and efficient at generating customers. You should be continually improving what you do, and now it's important to assess your strategic growth plans. Ask yourself at this point how to beat or evade the competition and how to increase the scale of your business. This tends to be a very critical moment because it's easy to get stuck and remain in your comfort zone. *How do I know if I've reached this point?* There's a high level of repeated sales from your customers. You find your customers seeking you out on a more continual basis. Your income flow is relatively stable, and you can plan your monthly or annual sales with greater precision. *What should I focus on?* At this stage, you should stop for a moment and seriously think about your business. What has worked? What hasn't worked? How should the future be? This is a pivotal time to plan for the future. Write your conclusions down about your startup in the notebook.

6–10 years after opening. By this time, your business should be functioning almost automatically. Your onsite presence might not be essential for proper management. Think about geographical expansion or on new products or markets, exit strategies, and succession plans. *How do I know if I've reached this point?* If you can be on the road for three months without having to stay in contact and the business stays on course, then that means you've arrived at this point. The business has a solid executive team and solid work plans. *What should I focus on?* A second strategic plan is recommended, although the goal is slightly different. By this time, you can decide whether to diversify geographically by product or line. Your business will have the capital to invest in other opportunities without running any risks. Write your conclusions down about your startup in the notebook.

As Eric Ries recommends in his book *Lean Startup*, during these phases it's vital to:

Build. Start selling and testing your product or service incurring in the lowest possible costs.

Measure. Validate recurring patterns. What works, and what could you do differently?

Learn. What can you adjust overall in the business model, and what can you learn from what you've observed? This is to be an endless cycle.

When I first met Brendon Burchard in Silicon Valley, author of many New York Times Best Sellers such as *The Millionaire Messenger* and *The Charge*, he made me question certain concepts of organizational structure by stating, "I hired my first employee when I made my first million in sales." He's been diligent in applying the principles set forth by Tim Ferris about automating his customer processes with tools such as InfusionSoft. Today, his business has 4 employees, billing over $10 million per year. The structure itself doesn't necessarily involve high fixed costs. In today's business world, this may mean cloud-based tools, software as a service (SAAS), co-workers around the globe and working from home instead of investing in costly office space. In short, this business structure is the most efficient way to achieve sustainable results. Technology today is causing us to question traditional forms of operating a business and seek better alternatives for achieving a functional business structure to support our undertaking.

People

The majority of people just ask and ask for more, yet very few times, if ever, do they check to see what they can offer.
— Anonymous

At this point in your business, we need to analyze two elements in relation to people:

- I as an entrepreneur and the roles I need to assume or assign to my team
- How to invite, develop, and retain personnel, as well as how to hire, compensate, and train

Element #1: The 3 Roles of an Entrepreneur

Michael Gerber is one of the authors that have most shifted my way of looking at a business. In his book *The E-Myth* he invites us to think about our business like a franchise. What processes can I systemize? Which can I delegate to technology?

Gerber starts off by questioning us as entrepreneurs and the three roles we should be fulfilling.

Manager: The one who administrates the undertaking

Visionary: The future of the undertaking

Technician: The one who knows to do what is vital and crucial to the undertaking.

Rarely if ever will you come across an entrepreneur with all three features developed. There are cases where a phenomenal technician turns into a poor businessman (e.g. a great baker with poor business skills), other cases where an excellent visionary turns into a bad businessperson (e.g. an inventor that jumps from project to project but never completes any of them), and there are also cases where a great manager turns into a poor businessperson (e.g. successful high-ranking executives that fail when they launch out individually). It's these unique properties that press us to form a key entrepreneurial team. Please answer the following questions in your notebook:

- Who's the visionary of the business?
- Who's the technician of the business?
- Who's the manager of the business?

There are times when one person can fulfill all three roles, but they're very unique and wearisome, hence the reason behind forming a solid team to meet those roles. There are no formulas for this part of the process since each business venture is different and each entrepreneurial team will have its own unique set of traits. What is paramount is that all three roles be present at all times.

Element #2: How do I hire and compensate?

You've heard time and again that the most important asset in a company is their people. I would like to add that the most important asset to a company is the *right* people. I always jest with people that hire me for a developmental process that if the goal is to climb a tree, then there are two options: hire squirrels or train turkeys. Sure you can train turkeys, but the process is going to be much more expensive than simply hiring squirrels in the first place. The same thing applies to new businesses when you don't seek out the right people to share the dream with. Many times entrepreneurs, to a certain degree, feel appreciative of people that would want to work with them. Often they aren't concerned with quality in the hiring process, but all they focus on is in filling the openings. By quality, I'm referring to the alignment of person-position-dream-passion-talent. You need to hire people that:

- Have a dream similar to yours
- Have a passion for the area they'll be assigned to
- Have a talent for the function they'll be performing

Every time I hire someone, I always ask him or her the following questions.

- How do you see yourself in the next 5 years?
- How do you see yourself in the next 15 years?
- What's your ideal job?
- What things are you passionate about?
- What are your talents?
- What things discourage you?
- If you had all the money in the world, what line of work would you be in?
- What has led you to change jobs in the past?

Moreover, I always verify references. A resume is a poor indicator of a person. I've yet to see a totally honest and sincere resume. No one writes, "I was laid off this job for not working the amount of hours I was hired to," or "I was fired for aggravated larceny." I always see embellished resumes where people list "being a perfectionist" as their greatest weakness. Take the time to call the previous companies for which the applicant has worked. Don't only check the personal contacts they include in their resume, but also call the companies and inquire about the new applicant from different people that knew him. My experience has been that when they decline to provide any references, it's a red flag to consider.

Believe me, I'm a person that deeply values others. People who know me know that I'm extremely approachable and people-oriented. However, I have great respect for the organization I run, and I take great care to ensure that new employees bring value to the company and the culture we're building. The same goes for us as an organization toward them, that we might also contribute toward the purpose that person has in life. Hiring new personnel should always be envisioned as a long-term relationship.

My first option when hiring new people is to check within my inner circle for professionals they might recommend. Normally, those that know me are aware of the type of people I'll feel most comfortable with. My best recruits have been a product of both, recommendations from people within the organization and referrals from people close to me.

Remember that it's these people who will help build your company by your side. They are your future leaders and managers within the business. We must apply the sound advice set forth by leadership writer John Maxwell: slow to hire and quick to fire.

Did you know that McDonald's purposefully hires people that smile? There's a process they have in the interview phase called the smile-o-meter, and it's designed to measure how many smiles the person makes in a set amount of time.

At Disney, any member of the cast can tell you exactly where you parked your vehicle by just asking a simple question, "What time did you get here?" This is all it takes for that person to take you to your exact parking space. Mr. Walt Disney always taught his people that the magic takes place when you place ordinary people in extraordinary processes.

How to hire the best candidates from the start

I can't stress enough the importance on hiring the right people. Additionally, the principle that "good draws on good" can easily be applied here as well. Your first workers will convey the mystique that you desire for your business, just like your first customers will determine your future ones. If you've already served three multinational companies, then it will be easy to cater to ten. However, if you've only served small businesses, then your natural preference will be for those. If you have competent people, they in turn will seek to draw more competent people. Drawing high-potential people to a startup will require your ability to sell ideas, which is also vitally important.

Recent studies have shown that money really isn't the number one motivator in people. I share this because perhaps many of you think that the reason you can't draw high-level people is because you can't pay them enough. Allow me to summarize what Daniel Pink discovered in his book *Drive: The Surprising Truth of What Motivates Us*. People require three elements to commit to a cause:

Purpose. Why am I doing this? What legacy am I leaving?

Autonomy. Can I contribute individually? Will I have liberty to do my job?

Sense of advancement. Will I make more if the business does better? Will I be able to see the fruit of my labor?

If you provide a person with these three elements, you'll most likely engage a more sustainable motivation in them. But if a person joins your undertaking just for the money, you'll end up with a very frustrated employee, and you'll want to get him out of your business as soon as possible. There's nothing more burdensome in a startup than to have people there just for a paycheck. On the other hand, you'll revel in having a team of people that believe in the same cause as you and who are there to see what you can build together. Money is simply a bonus, a consequence of a job well done.

Analyze your startup with the following questions:

- What is the purpose of your business?
- Why should anyone want to work with you?
- What opportunities of autonomy does my business provide?
- How will I provide a sense of advancement in my business?

Your compensation structure is the next point to consider. Everyone wants to feel secure with his or her income. Something you might encounter more often are fixed compensation systems. How about including commissions as incentives for your sales force? How about dividing a percentage of the profits among everyone? Stock options are a good practice, but it depends on legislation in your country. In some countries, adding new shareholders is a very complicated process.

The important thing is that regardless of what compensation system you use, make it a flexible one. I also speak a lot on how businesses should be meritocratic. Everywhere I go, people talk about creating a culture of ownership, of people that act like businesspeople, however they don't remunerate in the same manner. If you truly want a culture of owners, vary the pay so that everyone feels that they are contributing and receiving their dues from their contribution.

There are many indicators you can take into account when paying your key people. Payments based on generated marginal value or payments based on earnings taking into account capital costs (adjusting profits to a cutoff rate to make up for the cost of opportunity) are the trend. Each day, more and more business ventures seek to have a lower base than the part that's adjustable (for example 40 fixed/60 adjustable) to make sure that there's an alignment between what shareholders want and what workers in the business expect. The premise is simple. You as a businessman work more hours, so you're expecting not only your dream to become a reality, but to be able to capitalize on that work. Likewise, allow your team to dream with you also, permitting them to make more as the business moves forward.

Finally, another possible tool is deferred bonuses and results. For example, let's say you agreed to pay someone a $100 bonus. You could divide it throughout a 4-year plan, paying $25 per year and accruing the rest. This way the individual has an incentive to continue adding value and feels comfortable belonging to the business in order to capitalize on future bonuses.

Look at the following table. Let's suppose the person consistently reaches his goals, qualifying him for a $100 bonus.

YEAR	1	2	3	4
BONUS	25	25	25	25
		25	25	25
			25	25
				25
Total	25	50	75	100

In this table, the person has an adjustable income, but is also accruing for their future, just like the business owner who is making their business grow.

Of course, I'm assuming that you have the right person in place who shares the same vision for the business. However, if the person isn't the right one, then there's not enough money in the world to ever motivate him. Remember the simple logic behind incentives. There are two main motivators: intrinsic (those built into the job itself) and extrinsic (money, tangible benefits). If a job provides me with very few intrinsic motivators (I don't like the job), then I'll expect more extrinsic ones (more money). This is the reason why entrepreneurs tend to work so many more hours (high intrinsic motivator wanting to see their dream come alive) while receiving so little money at the start (low extrinsic motivator). Be passionate about your job, and you'll enjoy your wages even more at the end of the month for something you would have done anyway, for little or no pay. In your notebook, write down the current compensation package for you and your team.

Total amount	Fixed %	Adjustable %

Now write how your compensation package should be.

Total amount	Fixed %	Adjustable %

Also, you can always hire people at www.freelancer.com or www.zirtual.com when dealing with clearly defined job assignments.

What if I have a family business? How do I approach the people?

It's estimated that over 80% of businesses worldwide are family owned. It's a mistake to believe that a family business is synonymous with a small business. The ten largest family-owned businesses, in terms of annual billing, are Walmart, Ford Motor, Samsung, LG, Carrefour, Fiat, Ifi Instituto Finanziario Industriale S.p.A., PSA Peugeot Citroën S.A, Cargill, and BMW. Every one of them collects over $2 billion dollars in invoices per year (there are over 200 companies worldwide that meets this criterion).

However, it's not the norm that a family business is synonymous with growth and success. In fact, it's totally the opposite because 70% of family businesses either fail or are sold prior to the second generation. A mere 10% are still active by the third generation. There's even a saying in Mexico, "The store owner father, the knightly son, and the beggared grandson." While CEOs enjoy 6-year stints in public enterprises, family-owned businesses on average, enjoy tenures of up to 20–25 years, which tends to become an inconvenience. Are there any common patterns with those that fail? Can anything be done about it? George Stalk and Henry Foley have published a work in progress in the Harvard Business Review that may provide indicators of certain patterns.

Trap #1. "There will always be a place for you in the company." It's common to find that being closely related to the owner guarantees you a position in the company. It's also common to select relatives who lack the required skills for executive positions within the organization. Often the family business is viewed as the life jacket in case "something goes wrong in my professional career." Successful family enterprises have a clear-cut path to incorporating relatives in the business. Some make it a requirement for certain academic degrees, years of experience in outside businesses, or working in positions available with real needs and openings. I recall the president of a highly successful family business once say, "My children don't own anything yet. The only thing they can be sure of by being a member of this family is their college tuition and to later be able to opt, should they wish so and qualify as well, for a position in the family business."

Has my business fallen prey to this trap? Think about it, and write it down in your notebook.

Trap #2. "As the family grows, the business will also." Most often than not, families grow at a quicker pace than does a business. The number of children, grandchildren, nieces, nephews, sons-in-law, and daughters-in-law continues to grow. If the company hasn't clearly defined the process mentioned above, it runs the risk of becoming an employment agency and no longer an organization that adds long-term value to those who serve in it.

I remember a student in a master's program saying in class, "I really don't have to get good grades because I've always got my dad's business to fall back on." Can you imagine if every one of our loved ones thought this way? There'd be no business that would ever have enough positions for everyone. Successful corporations always regulate the incorporation of loved ones into the business, not just with meritocratic controls, but also with family growth strategy alignments. In other words, they foresee within future plans any specific openings and positions where qualified family members can exercise their leadership skills. Has my business fallen prey to this trap? Analyze and write it down in your notebook.

Trap #3. "Creating relationship silos." There are businesses that fall into the trap of allotting specific positions for people with certain last names. In fact, there are even entire departments, units, or areas that are commandeered under this criterion. Successful businesses apply meritocratic measures, combined with a healthy practice of assigning external mentors with real authority over the apprentice. Wisdom is found in the multitude of counselors. Has my business fallen prey to this trap? Analyze and write it down in your notebook.

Starting a new venture is indeed exciting, and doing so in a family can be even more so. How do you solve the potential rivalry between love and money? The key is found in aligning your expectations from the start and applying good practices throughout.

Did you know that Zappos offers all new workers in the company a $2,000 bonus and one-week's pay for resigning. Yet, in spite of how attractive the offer may be, 97% of people stay with the company. This practice reinforces the principle mentioned earlier: slow to hire and quick to fire. Zappos clearly knows that any new worker that doesn't align to their unique workflow will end up being more harmful than the amount paid in the exit bond.

Culture - How to define my organization's DNA

This is the third aspect to take into account when talking about a business undertaking making strides because it is no longer the dream of one individual alone, but has now become a viable project involving many people. Let's look at how three emblematic corporations define their DNA.

At Apple we:

- Simplify
- Perfect
- Amaze

At Zappos we:

- Provide the WOW through our service
- Embrace and promote change
- Have fun and are a little eccentric
- Are adventurous, creative, and open-minded
- Pursue knowledge and growth
- Develop open and honest lines of communication
- Build a positive group with a spirit of family
- Do more with less
- Are passionate and determined with what we do
- Are humble

At Disney:

- Innovation: We are committed to a tradition of innovation and technology.
- Quality: We strive to maintain a high level of excellence and standards in all our products and services.
- Community: We create positive ideas for the family. We provide enriching and entertaining experiences for people of all generations to share in.
- Storytelling: Timeless and inviting stories that both delight and inspire.

- Optimism: Entertainment around hope, aspiration, and positive results.
- Correctness: We honor and respect the trust people place in our hands. Fun is about laughing at our own experiences and ourselves as well.

Are the previous statements effective at describing the people and work environment in their businesses? What would our core business values sound like?

What traits should we look for in people to make them part of the DNA of our culture?

McClelland coined the term "competencies" to define individual traits that could predict performance. Much evidence has been found to support the notion that selecting, developing, and retaining personnel with the right competencies for a business are high indicators of success for the organization. Therefore, an organization's DNA refers to the model of attributes or competencies that people in that particular company should have.

Competencies are made up of three components: attitudes (what I want to do), skills (what I can do), and knowledge (what I know how to do).

There are businesses where just a suspicion of sexual harassment is grounds for immediate dismissal without any major investigation into the matter. However, there are other companies where unfortunately it's totally the opposite, and these situations are common in their corporations. They are taboos that everyone's aware of, but no one does anything about it. All these behaviors form part of an organization's DNA. They mold your culture and the type of people that work in it.

What do people do when it's time to clock out? What are the bosses' offices like? Where do people park their vehicles? Are there pictures of the founders in specific areas of the workplace? What subjects can you joke about? Are you allowed to talk about God at your workplace? Are there more task-oriented or people-oriented leaders? All of these elements make up your business culture. It's not something that happens overnight, but once set, changing it takes time. Although it's qualitative in nature, in other words you can "feel the culture," it's also directly related to the business's financial outcome, as well as to the venture's sustainability.

I'll never forget the reply McDonald's Patty Cofiño gave me when I asked her what they do to have so many workers smile on such a consistent basis. The answer was quite simple. "We only hire people that smile." As I've mentioned before, to them it's a decisive factor in their culture of service, which leads us to meditate now on the process following the hiring phase. It's crucial. How do I start defining the desired culture in my startup? Usually one can deem as better practices those used at AT&T or Phillip Morris International, since all of their processes in relation to people are based on competencies, making sure that people have the desired attitude, the right knowledge, and the optimum skills required.

Now in terms of what is easier or more complex to develop, let's look at the following table:

Component	Developmental process level of difficulty	Notes	Example
Attitudes (what I want to do)	High	The hiring process of dominant attitudes is much easier. Literature shows that modifying attitudes is possible, however it requires constant reinforcement in structured processes, as well as continual coaching and mentoring. All of these activities are costlier in terms of time and money.	McDonald's hiring process measures the amount of smiles in a set period of time to ensure the right attitude.

Skills (what I can do)	Medium	The key to this process is reinforcement and on-site training. An alternative can be controlled learning capsules.	Process training is divided into daily-reinforcement cards, combined with a "lead peer" that teaches, trains, and reinforces what is learned.
Knowledge (what I know how to do)	Low	The key lies in specific function and position-based knowledge aligned to the desired culture.	McDonald's has a highly structured, positional induction program and capsules of cognitive learning components laid out throughout key areas in the restaurants.

For a number of years, much has been said about competency modeled processes in organizations. Corporate universities have become popular in transferring a particular business's universe of knowledge to all of its employees. Specific entrepreneurial training programs have been designed to reinforce the desired attitudes, knowledge, and skills you want in them. Once again, the key to these new programs is found in understanding the strategy, the basic cause for the undertaking, the essence of the business, and the mystique that the founders wish to permeate throughout the company. This in turn is reinforced by hiring new people, by rewards and reprimands, by what is talked about on a daily basis, and by what is followed up on in the business.

After looking at these concepts, ask yourself the following questions. Copy and answer them in your notebook.

In order to guarantee the success of my business:

- What attitudes do I need?
- What knowledge is required?
- What basic skills do I need?

- How do you define the essence of the people I'm seeking to hire?
- What are the non-negotiables?

Think about your business for a moment and about some of your current cultural components and about those you desire. Copy and fill in the following table in your notebook.

Element	How is it now?	How would I like it to be?
Visible symbols (offices, parking lot, images, decoration, etc.)		
Values		
Communication		
Heroes (who do we reward)		
Villains (who do we reprimand)		
Basic core beliefs		
What do we talk about every day?		
Compensation system (how do we pay our people)		
Policies		
Code of ethics		
Types of customers we cater to		

Which of these cultures would you like to have in your undertaking?

Figure 1: Framework of Competitive Values. Cameron and Quinn (2006)

How to create a culture of accountability

One of the keys to a new business undertaking is the discipline of following up on things. It's common for founders to have a clear vision of what they'll do and how to bring it to pass; however, many times there's a tendency to expect the people working with them to know what that is and how to do it automatically. How can our fellow workers follow up on assignments that haven't been conveyed clearly? This is the reason why clear and effective communication must be a core element in your business culture.

Additionally, in the first stages of a business, there's so much that needs to be done that the to-do lists can quickly pile up. As a new entrepreneur, you've already experienced what it's like to have many bosses (every customer, every supplier, every shareholder) and how everything—and I mean *everything*—appears to be urgent. The phone's not working? You fix it. There's no money? You fix it. Customers haven't paid? You fix it. No money in the account? You fix it. Need a website? You fix it. So how do you balance the strategic (which is crucial) with the day-to-day execution (which is also vital)?

The answer is simple, but putting it into practice can be difficult. Prioritize and delegate. Yes, I know you're thinking that you don't have anyone to whom you can delegate, but little by little you'll put your team together and learn to delegate. Always engage in weekly follow-ups with them.

One of the best practices you can ever have is holding accountability sessions every week. Get together with your team anywhere from 45 minutes to 1 hour (regardless if it's just you and your partner or your first fellow worker), and follow up on everything you had set to complete the week before and how those tasks affect the vision, long-term strategy, and overall achievement of your purpose. If you don't have any workers yet, it's healthy to meet with your mentors and inform them of your progress. The important thing is to:

- Have an outline of your five-year, one-year and weekly plans
- Have clear, set goals for the week, the month, and the year

- Take notes of what is said and agreed on
- Follow up closely on everything agreed on

If you've noticed, many of the recommendations in this book are aimed at helping you plan more effectively. However, there's another part dedicated to executing it. Trust me when I tell you that in my personal life this was quite a challenge. I expected people, as if by osmosis, to know what I was thinking, and I would get upset when they didn't follow up on what was agreed to. It was logical because we didn't schedule periodic meetings to reinforce what was important.

On a personal note, I enjoy writing, teaching, and designing more than looking at all the details a new business entails. However, just because I don't like it, that doesn't mean it's not important. The business has grown in leaps and bounds from the moment I made up my mind to make these principles part of our core culture.

Was I the one that changed? No. But I have many more people on my team whose strengths are administration and the discipline to see things through. I continue to contribute the things I love, but I enjoy even more seeing how things continue to advance thanks to my team's work. Now we can react more quickly to any crisis, and high-demand projects can have much closer follow-throughs. It's not the same thing to find out one day before a payment's due that we're out of money, then to have cash flows up to date and allot the necessary expenditures ahead of time. Choose to make accountability a vital element of your business's culture. Read the following questions, and answer them in your notebook.

- What are you measuring in your business?
- How often do you measure it?
- Who's keeping the minutes of everything that's agreed upon?
- How do you follow up on everything that's agreed upon?
- To whom are you accountable?

I always say that this process is like losing weight. It's not until you choose to measure your weight on a weekly basis with someone holding you accountable that you start to take it seriously. But if no one's aware of it, I can easily slip and say, "No one's going to notice a few extra pounds on me." You'll find more on accountability and execution toward the end of this book.

Founder of the Entrepreneur's Organization (EO), Verne Hanish, in his book *Mastering the Rockefeller Habits*, shares insights on how to plan in just one page. I believe this outline is a powerful tool for the different variables we need to follow up on for the rest of our life, not to mention making them an intricate part of your business culture—Us, Inc.

Accountability

TIME FRAME		
Daily	Schedule	Who
Weekly	Schedule	When
Quarterly	Actions	How
Annually	Goals	What
3-5 Years	Targets	Where
Life of Leader	Purpose	Why
Forever	Core Values	Should

All of Us, Inc. 3

If I were given a chance to set a world record, it would be that I have 150 partners, all with their own flourishing businesses, that started out with nothing and we made the difference in their lives, turning them into millionaires.
– Barbara Corcoran

Positive Impact Multiplier

In 2006, Blake Mycoskie traveled to Argentina and encountered a number of barefoot children. Desiring to help them, Mycoskie founded TOMS Shoes, a business dedicated to donating one pair of shoes for every pair sold.

This American entrepreneur returned to Argentina with family and friends to donate over 100,000 pairs of shoes for children in need to a local NGO named LIFE. The company designs and sells light footwear based on an Argentinian Alpargata's design.

TOMS Shoes was created with a specific mission in mind: donate shoes in accordance to their sales. Thanks to this philosophy, the shoes designs turn into benefactors, an element that helps the business grow with strong sustainable roots.

Imagine that your business is successful and creates the impact you desired. Are you happy now? Let's look at some statistics of people that have gone through those same stages of success.

Enemy #1
It's More Difficult to
Manage Success Than Failure

Enemy #2
An Entrepreneur's Strong
Point is also His Weakness

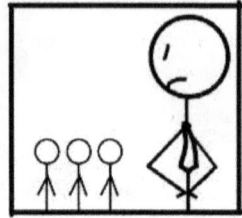

Enemy #3
From a Noble Vision
to a Tyrannical One

- The average millionaire goes broke at least 3.5 times in their lifetime.
- Only 20% of millionaires ever retire. Over 80% of them still get up to work every morning.
- Carlos Slim Helu, Mexican billionaire with a vast fortune estimated at 69 billion dollars, is considered the very first "world's richest man" from a country in development. He's lived in the same modest house for the last 30 years. His wealth is equivalent to 5% of Mexico's economy, making close to $30 million a day.
- Billionaire Bill Gates announced that he was going to donate his fortune, estimated at $61 billion, to charity, leaving a maximum of $10 million for each of his three children. Warren Buffet has decided to do the same.
- There are approximately 1,226 billionaires worldwide. Women make up 8.5% of them.
- In 2008, there were approximately 10 million people classified as millionaires in U.S. dollars.

According to Oxfam's research for 2015:

- 48% of the world's wealth is in 1% of the population
- It's estimated to grow to 50% by 2016

In contrast:

- Over 80% of the less wealthy hold only 5.5% of the world's total wealth

What do these statistics tell us?

- Success isn't an overnight occurrence. It often requires going through multiple failures.
- The goal of those that have made fortunes isn't to retire, but to find satisfaction in what they do.
- Having money doesn't mean losing sight of daily expenses.
- There are cases where all of the amassed fortune will end up donated.
- There are multiple cases of millionaires and billionaires.
- We have an enormous challenge before us when it comes to wealth distribution.

And this is the challenge I call *All of Us, Inc.* Entrepreneurship isn't about an I or even Us, but it's about All of Us, Inc. How can we help create a more sustainable, prosperous, and abundant world?

What's keeping you from going from success to transcendence in your business? What's holding you back from impacting your environment by modeling positive leadership roles? In the end, entrepreneurship is a collective activity for the common good. And that's what our projections should be about. However, there are certain enemies we need to overcome in the process.

Enemies to Overcome

All of Us, Inc.'s Enemy #1: It's more difficult to manage success than failure

A very relevant topic that never goes out of date is human behavior—those attitudes that vary with time and those that will remain the same. Have you ever stopped to notice how many successful leaders today lose it all because of self-destructive behaviors? Why does it happen so often? There are countless examples today of people that are elevated to high leadership positions and end up sabotaging themselves: managers, businesspeople, religious leaders, politicians, academics, and artists. In 1989, Manfred F.R. Kets de Vries published some ideas that can help shed light on this.

In many case studies, Kets de Vries discovered at least three common causes for self-destructive behaviors: isolation from reality, transference from followers, and fear of success.

Let's look at each one.

Isolation from Reality. When assuming a leadership role, it's normal to hear things like "You've got to keep your distance." And culturally speaking, Latin America tends to mark great distances between levels of power, accentuating this prescription (between leader and follower or boss and subordinate). Naturally, by doing this, leaders start to lose their grip on reality missing out on the following: first-hand information from customers or fellow workers closest to him, informal feedback from colleagues or peers, and more. Then, of course, isolation from reality can easily lead to decision-making based on faulty premises. As an entrepreneur, how are you in this respect?

Transference from followers. Failure in leaders is many times intricately connected to the followers themselves. There's a natural predisposition in followers to look for infallibility in their leaders, to look for that security and psychological reaffirmation we used to find in our parents' idyllic roles. For example, why is it that in times of crisis there's an automatic reemergence of people that say yes to everything? It's precisely because in times of insecurity, we subconsciously turn to others outside of us to provide us with security, resolve, and peace of mind. We end up denying our leaders timely, honest feedback until it's too late. As an entrepreneur, how are you in this respect?

Fear of success. This cause might seem contradictory, but there is indeed an intrinsic fear of success in many of us. We all want to be successful, but we tend to entertain thoughts such as, "What if I lose it all," "What if it changes me for the worse," "Why do I deserve this level of success?" These thoughts in turn automatically spark destructive, compensatory behaviors on the success itself. As an entrepreneur, how are you in this respect?

In spite of these causes, what can we do to avoid succumbing to success?

Humility. Recognize that you're not the only author of your success. You're human, and you make mistakes. In spite of this, the fragility of the messenger in no way diminishes the power of the message.

Be accessible. Allow people to approach you and share their concerns. Speak directly to your customers, suppliers, and fellow workers.

Elicit feedback. Understand that bad news isn't a personal vendetta against you, nor is it to criticize you. Accept the information that will allow you to adjust the vision. Don't take it personally when things don't turn out the way you expect them to in an organization. Foster discussions and roundtables to collect reliable information.

Get enough rest. If you're overworked, your propensity to fail is greater. Sometimes it's not easy to rest, but just as you take the time to schedule meetings, you must also take the time to schedule rest periods. How are you as an entrepreneur in these four aspects?

Aspect	Yes	No	What would people who know me say about this?
Am I humble?			
Am I accessible (approachable)?			
Do I look for honest, transparent feedback?			
Do I schedule enough time to rest?			

Look at the explanation Jim Collins has to offer concerning this:

Imagine getting two World Guinness records. One for the greatest number of followers in the shortest amount of time on the popular social media known as Twitter: one million followers in 25 hours and 17 minutes, and another for getting the highest compensation per TV episode: $1.25 million. Of course, we're talking about Charlie Sheen, from the popular hit TV series *Two and a Half Men*. Controversy has always surrounded Sheen, who in fits of rage insulted the series production team, made derogatory statements about our Savior, lost the right to see his children due to domestic violence, and boasted in knowing exactly "how to get high." He has even gone as far as to say that only "losers die from drug overdoses." In just a few days he polarized the entire public, from those who lost every last bit of respect for the actor, to those that set him up as their new role model. My question to you is, what can lead a person from the apex of their success to commit such acts as to place his life in danger as well of those of his family and his career?

The majority of writers, as mentioned earlier, agree that everything points back to pride. Jim Collins states in his work, *How the Mighty Fall*, that the first phase of failure is the haughtiness that is birthed from success. The Bible also clearly delineates this principle in Proverbs 16:18, "Pride comes before destruction and a conceited spirit before a fall." Using pride as a foundation, let's look at three additional causes that can easily turn into three temptations when you reach success.

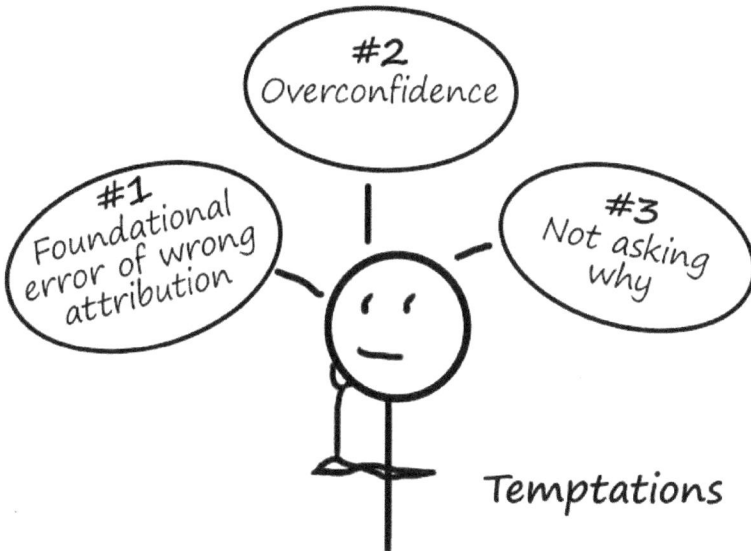

Temptation #1: Foundational error of wrong attribution. This is the term psychologists refer to as the phenomenon of ascribing our success to our own individual abilities, without taking into account random, aleatory events or the involvement of outsiders. To what do we attribute success? To us alone or to all of the events that made it possible? In your notebook, list all of the factors that have led you to be successful?

Temptation #2: Overconfidence. Success breeds confidence in our skills and our abilities. This alone isn't negative; however, the possibility of carelessly undertaking new challenges or of taking unnecessary risks does greatly increase. Do I carefully examine my strengths as well as my areas of opportunity? Do I clearly identify what areas might be difficult to manage once I experience success?

In your notebook, list your main strengths and weaknesses as an entrepreneur.

Temptation #3: Not asking why. Whenever we achieve success, we normally don't question it. However, when failure hits, it's a different story. We're always asking ourselves, "Why did this happen to me?" It's paramount that we analyze and question success as well, and jot down why we think we've achieved it and what factors contributed toward it.

Why have I become successful? What are the reasons and factors behind it?

It's common to quote John F. Kennedy's famous phrase, "Success has many fathers, but failure is an orphan." Reaching success is fulfilling (although its definition is individual and subjective), yet what's most important is making it sustainable without causing harm to others in the process.

All of Us, Inc.'s Enemy #2: An entrepreneur's strong point is also his weakness

Entrepreneurs have many positive traits. Yet, there are some underlying features that could prove ominous for the person, their business, and the people around them. There's a dark side to them. Manfred F.R. Kets de Vries researched some of these interesting features.

What are you like?

Entrepreneurs are achievement oriented. They love having to be responsible for complex decision-making processes, and they hate routine and repetitive work. They are especially creative, possessing high levels of energy, perseverance, and imagination. These attributes, combined with a disposition for taking calculated risks, allow them to transform what barely starts off as an idea into something solid. Entrepreneurs are wired to inspire a high level of contagious enthusiasm within an organization. They instill a high sense of purpose while at the same convincing others that they're exactly where the action is at. Regardless of the trait—be it charisma, a pleasant personality, players who bet to win—entrepreneurs to a certain degree know how to lead an organization and give it the boost it needs.

Yet along with that mystique, entrepreneurs can have certain aspects of their personality that make them difficult to work with. For example, their push toward action many times leads them to appear to act senselessly, not giving it much thought, while causing a great impact on organizations. On other occasions, entrepreneurs can fall prey to not accepting suggestions or taking advice, which in turn can also lead to catastrophic mistakes for the organization.

So is there a dark side to an entrepreneur? Let's look at three common features and bear in mind that these are inclinations, hence not all entrepreneurs are alike.

The need for control. Common phrases that resonate among entrepreneurs are, "I'm a bad employee, because I just can't have a boss," or "I can do it better than my boss, so I'll just go into business for myself." It's common to observe a high level of control among entrepreneurs. It turns them into chiefs wanting to control everything—from the smallest detail in an organization to everything that happens within it and its employees. They're distrustful of coworkers that take initiative or that don't convey their actions well, causing them to feel they're losing control. In many cases, new businesses arise from people that are "rebels with a cause" that don't find a place to express their creativity and individual talents in the organizational structures of the day. As with everything in life, this and the following features can be either good or bad, depending on its moderate or extreme use. How do I measure up in this aspect?

Feeling of distrust. Entrepreneurs have learned to be distrustful. They are distrustful of those that inquire about their business (vaguely answering with phrases such as "more or less" or "hanging in there"), of the competition, of their closest associates, and of the world in general. They're always in fear of people stealing things if they are not under their control, of spies from the competition, or of a key partner taking their business away. The curious thing is that many times they're actually right. In an odd way, it's a type of self-fulfilling prophecy. In any company, if we dig deep enough, we'll always find something that's off. Once again, going to the extreme is the risky part. If this distrust paralyzes the organization or causes it to lose key talent, then extra care has to be taken. How do I measure up in this aspect?

The need for praise. Entrepreneurs wish to be heroes. They wish to be mythical heroes that start from scratch, overcome every obstacle, and reach the top. The risk involved in making great conquests, in overcoming great forces, and in defeating the foes along the way, reinforces the feeling of control and distrust and breeds the need for more praise. Entrepreneurs yearn to be acknowledged for their victories. On many occasions, they even erect monuments for their achievements (great and luxurious buildings that don't necessarily help toward the purpose of the business itself), or they seek the recognition of others. This is normal; after all, they've beaten many others to the finish line. However, it's the extremes that you need to watch out for. How do I measure up in this aspect?

Did you identify with any of the traits you need to watch out for? What do you plan to do in this respect?

All of Us, Inc.'s Enemy #3: From a noble vision to a tyrannical one

Is my vision as an entrepreneur positive or ominous?

There are many people that use the privilege of serving others as a means to manipulate and reach their own personal objectives. We all desire to be leaders; however, often we don't fathom the dimensions of the responsibilities required within a leadership role. Just one word from us can damage the most basic beliefs of a human being, and one word can instill courage and inspiration into others. How can I tell if my business vision and my entrepreneurial leadership style are getting sidetracked? Are there any red flags?

Go over both your business vision and your personal vision. Ask yourself the following questions designed to help you identify possible danger signs to avoid.

- Is your vision noble and positive for you and your group but detrimental for others?

- Does the vision promise to make you great at the expense of making others little?
- Does the vision set you as the savior-leader that destroys every enemy or competitor?
- Does the vision necessarily require destroying your competition or anyone else in the process?
- Will your vision be able to bear the scrutiny of time and history?

Analyze yourself as a leader and answer the following questions.

- Are you showing signs of excessive pride or arrogance?
- Are you only getting advice from people that flatter you and say yes to everything you say?
- Do you use other people for your dirty work and then turn your back on them?
- Do you look down on the weakest members of the team?
- Do you blame others for your decisions or deeds?
- Do you act for your own personal gain, above everyone else's?
- Do you disguise questionable deeds with altruism and nobility?

The first step to develop as a person and as a leader is to know your baseline. Where are you right now? Are you getting the results you're expecting as a leader or person? Do you have accountability measures set in place for your progress as a leader and as a person?

Positive, transformational leadership is possible. Leaders such as Alfred P. Sloan Jr., Martin Luther King Jr., Aaron Feuerstein, Nelson Mandela, Anita Roddick, Gandhi, Desmond Tutu, and Vaclav Havel have inspired us to greatness and to move the world forward. Notwithstanding, these results are less frequent than we desire. Perhaps it's because we are taught how to be leaders, but not how to be followers and put a demand on good leadership.

Are you ready to ask yourself those difficult questions? If you've found areas that you need to improve, are you willing to do something about it? The practice of effective leadership starts within our own selves.

What have I discovered? How will I proceed?

To end this section on self-awareness, it pays to periodically seek the advice of mentors. Do you have other entrepreneurs that can counsel you?

Don't seek one same person for everything. Remember, we need to find mentors in specific areas. Seek out the best spiritual leaders to help you in spiritual matters. Seek out the best administrators to help you in matters of organization. Ask the best salesmen on how to promote the commercial area in your business.

Write down the names of at least ten mentors that can help you.

Mentor's Name	Expertise

From I, Inc. to All of Us, Inc.

What will I do now?

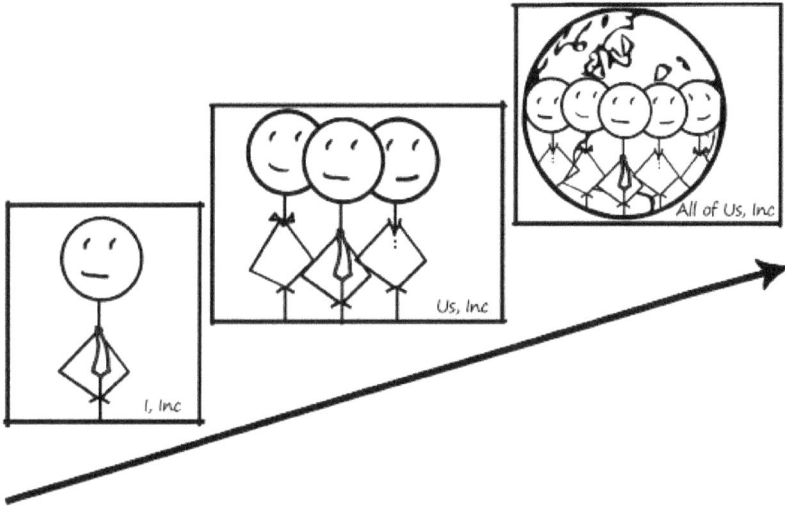

"This year, yes! Thanks to this book I'm going to start my own venture. This time, yes," you might say.

Here's an interesting piece of data: According to studies published in the *Harvard Business Review*, only 8% of people that set New Year's resolutions actually fulfill them. A study published in January 2010 showed that only 15% of Guatemalans actually plan and only 3% of them put it into writing. Now what can we do to improve our chances of reaching the goals we set our mind to? In order to become successful leaders in business with a positive impact in society, we need to plan, set goals, and conscientiously and objectively assess where we are right now. I know it seems like a simple subject to deal with, yet it's so vast and so powerfully influential throughout all aspects of life that it still never ceases to amaze me, especially when it comes to a business one has dreamt about, launched, and grown over time. Indeed, it's deserving of good and effective strategizing.

Research done by many universities throughout the U.S. and Europe, as well as data compiled by GLOBE (Global Studies of Culture and Leadership) of which Guatemala is a part of, consistently show that the executions of plans are heavily breached worldwide. Let's look at the statistics again. Of the people that set goals for the following year, only 8% actually reach them, 19% are successful though they take over a year, 49% have little success in achieving them, and 24% never ever reach their goals. However, when they were asked if they thought they would be successful, an overwhelming 52% answered yes, they would. So what is happening?

A closer examination of what many of these goals focus on shows that 47% of them are aimed at education or personal improvement, 38% have to do with weight loss, 34% have to do with money, and 31% have to do with relationships.

What do *your* goals focus on?

Upon closer inspection of which people are more likely to reach their goals, statistics show that out of all those who reached them, 39% were in their 20s and 15% were in their 50s. In other words, age does play a role in the prediction of goal achievement.

Why measure them? In planning, it's vital to clearly understand what the baseline is, the initial probability. Why is there such a large breach when it comes to execution? Let's look at three of the main causes.

Not really wanting to reach the goal. Often goals are set according to social pressures or what is socially acceptable in the goal maker's mind. If the goal isn't relevant to you and you're not passionate about it, then you'll never reach it. The first key is in making up your mind to do it. A firm decision is a well-worn path to reaching a desired result.

Setting too many ambiguous goals. It's common to want to set many general goals. For example, "losing weight" isn't a valid goal because you could lose just an ounce during the year and you'll have reached your goal. Goals should be set no more than three at a time, and they should be specific. Dropping three pounds per month and adding two in muscle mass is much better than the all too common "losing weight." If you set more than three goals, then classify them by dates. For example, three this month, three the next, and so on. Beyond that, they'll be hard to reach. The same thing applies to strategies in an organization.

Lacking an accountability system. Who else knows of your goals? Do you have a control chart to see your progress? Others must be informed of your goals for the year, and you must be responsible with checking them periodically. Perhaps you can schedule to check up on them every week and set up activities that will help you reach them. It's quite the thrill every time you know you're getting closer to your goal.

Planning is vital since, statistically speaking, you'll be six to ten times more likely to reach your dreams. Share your dreams with others, also. Set up accountability measures. Now write your conclusions and how they apply to your undertaking.

How will you define your success as an entrepreneur?

A few months ago, I started giving classes on strategy for the MBA program of a business school. I'm passionate about the class. It's not just about looking at businesses and how to make them more cost-effective, but it's about the way you see life itself. I always invite the students to hold off making any business strategies until they first lay out a strategy for their life.

During class we speak about success, but I dedicate a similar amount of time talking about failure. We share our experiences, and I always open up about mine, such as the time I had to stop and think about what really mattered in life when at the age of 26 I was hospitalized for a stress-related crisis. It's not easy feeling vulnerable, facing problems that I should not have had to face until much later in life. If you think about it, life is much like a business in the sense that I get a return for whatever resources I put into it. In my personal case, I had invested all of my time into work and the consequences were quite clear.

In class, the main subject of our discussions is around scorecards, metrics, and how to measure a strategy's execution. Therefore, I'd like to take the liberty to ask you the following questions: What metrics are you using to measure your life? How will you ultimately define success?

During the last World Business Forum in New York, my attention was drawn to the fact that the only speech that had receive a standing ovation was the one by Nando Parrado, survivor of the 1972 Andes airplane accident. His conclusion was, "We must have a purpose in life that goes beyond just making money."

Consequently, I read in the *Harvard Business Review* that among their most widely quoted articles was the one written by Clayton M. Christensen titled, "How will you measure your life?" The conclusion was clear: We are living in a world where external abundance keeps us from living a life full of purpose. We've immersed ourselves in a culture full of "having" but not "being." We spend little to no time meditating or working on our priorities. And to make things worse, we spend too much time criticizing others instead of reflecting on who we really are.

Who can really say what perfection is. I don't believe anyone can; yet we constantly demand it from others without being able to provide it ourselves. It's easy to say, "If I were managing that business, I'd do it this way," or see someone else's life and go, "How could they do that!" Yet rarely, if ever, do we dare to say, "What can I do right now to improve my quality of life" or "What am I really doing to have a positive impact on the lives of others, of those around me?"

When we speak about strategy, the foundational premise is that we only reap what we invest resources in. I'm not speaking only about money, but about time, focus, and energy. In other words, it's all about priorities. I've asked a number of people what their priorities are in life and the majority answer the same thing: God and their family. However, when I ask them how much time they invest into each one of those, the answers are almost always the same, "Not much, don't have time, I've got to work." So then what really is our priority? It's a subject that I have to face in my own life as well. I'd be lying if I said that I always do what's strategically correct in life. Yet, taking the time to consider the matter and doing something about it helps bring about a change in attitude.

What are you measuring in your business? How do you measure life?

A second strategically foundational premise is that you can only get what you are willing to measure. This is the reason behind setting key performance indicators (KPIs) and formal accountability systems. If we constantly assess our business's EBIT (earnings before interest and tax), margin, sales, and turnover rate to determine our company's level of performance, then why not apply the same principles to our life as well?

I was blown away by something Clayton Christiansen wrote in one of his articles. He shares, "God isn't going to measure my life by the amount of dollars I make, but by how many lives I touch." So then it's really not about prominence, status, or achievements but about helping others develop a better life. How will I be measured? How will my family measure me? My friends? My colleagues? Society?

I'm passionate about designing strategy, but more so when it's a life strategy where the metrics we measure and design will help build a better world for others.

Ask yourself the following questions.

- How do I define success?
- How do I measure if I'm being successful?
- What activities am I doing that contribute toward this result?
- Who do I ask feedback from?

My desire is for you to ask yourself the right questions that will challenge you to press on as a human being. Our world is in dire need of healthy leaders. Remember that a wounded leader hurts other as well. We can't expect our nation to prosper with leaders shifting the blame and not genuinely focused on building better businesses, better communities, and a better society as a whole.

If you want to change the world, then change yourself.
– Gandhi

Epilogue

As I beheld the plains before me, I decided that my fear of freedom would swiftly be replaced by the responsibility of my calling. I knew the truth. I couldn't sit idly by.

There were millions of people in that cavern, perhaps billions. I couldn't see them, nor could I ever meet them all, or wait. Perhaps yes, somehow.

You can slay the dreamer, but never the dream, I thought to myself, still fearful but daring to take this newfound liberty back with me.

Today I would define my purpose as a dream deliverer. I would inspire people to be the best version of themselves. I would show them that they had the power to take control of their lives.

And so I made my way back to the cavern with a renewed understanding, deciding to become the change I was longing to see in this world.

ADDITIONAL MATERIAL CONSULTED

1. Bygrave, William; Zacharakism Andrew (2004). *The Portable MBA in Entrepreneurship.* U.S., Wiley.

2. Collins, Jim (2002). *From Good to Great.* Colombia: Group Editorial Norma.

3. Herrmann, Ned (1996). *The Whole Brain Business Book.* U.S., McGraw Hill.

4. Hisrich, Robert; Peters, Michael; Shepherd, Dean (2009). *Entrepreneurship.* U.S., McGraw Hill (7th Edition).

5. Kim, Chan W., Mauborgne, Renée. (2005). *Blue Ocean Strategy.* Boston: Harvard Business School Press.

6. Porras, Emery, Thompson (2007). *Success Built to Last.* U.S., Pearson Education.

7. Shane, Scott (2008). *The Illusions of Entrepreneurship.* U.S., Yale University Press.

8. Zelaya, Julio (2009). *Hecho en Guatemala: Crónicas de Emprendimiento y Éxito.* Guatemala: The Learning Group Press.

9. http://www.infomipyme.com/

10. http://www.passioncatalyst.com/

11. http://www.infomipyme.com/Docs/GT/Offline/inicioempresa/descubrirooportunidadnegocios.html (Recursos para emprendedores de MIPYMES, Ministerio de Economía de Guatemala.)

ABOUT THE AUTHOR

He is the co author of the best sellers SuccessOnomics with Steve Forbes and Transform with Brian Tracy. He has shared stages as keynote speaker with Dave Ulrich, Peter Diamandis, Mark Victor Hansen, Henry Cloud, among others. He is a Principal at The RBL Group in the United States and Founder and President of Emprende U (www.emprendeu.com).

He holds a Post Doctorate in Management and Marketing from Tulane University, an MBA from INCAE Business School and certificates in entrepreneurship from Harvard University, Babson College, MIT, and Cornell University. He is a fellow of the Central American Leadership Initiative -CALI– of The Aspen Institute and member of the Aspen Global Leadership Network and a member of EO (Entrepreneur's Organization).

His work has been seen in ABC, NBC, CBS, E!, and FOX, as well as in the main Latin-American mass media. Speaker at TEDx with his talk "El Regalo de Soñar", "The Gift of Dreaming". He is a visiting scholar at Highpoint University, Penn State University, and Tulane University.

Member of the advisory board of Estrategia y Negocios, Central America's top business journal. Columnist at Siglo XXI, with his column "El Poder de Emprender", "The Power of Entrepreneurship". He advises more than 150 organizations in the United States, Latin America, and The Caribbean, training more than 100,000 people per year in live events and more than 500,000 people in digital media.

9 781941 142929